Everyday Cheapskate: Frugal Tips for Everyday Living

Everyday Cheapskate: Frugal Tips for Everyday Living

Mary Hunt

Creators Publishing
Hermosa Beach, CA

Everyday Cheapskate: Frugal Tips for Everyday Living

Cover art by Kelly Evans

CREATORS PUBLISHING
737 3rd St
Hermosa Beach, CA 90254
310-337-7003

ISBN (print): 978-1-949673-75-3
ISBN (ebook): 978-1-949673-66-1

First Edition
Printed in the United States of America
1 3 5 7 9 10 8 6 4 2

A Note From the Publisher

Since 1987, Creators has syndicated many of your favorite columns to newspapers. In this digital age, we are bringing collections of those columns to your fingertips. This will allow you to read and reread your favorite columnists, with your own personal digital archive of their work.

—Creators Publishing

Contents

Introduction

People call me a cheapskate, and contrary to what you might assume, I like it! It reminds me that I'm not who I used to be: a credit card junkie. Yes, I've come a long way since the days I plunged my family so deeply into debt there seemed to be no way we would ever get out. But we did. And I learned that living below one's means is an art, a way of life and a discipline that can be learned.

Just as I five- and ten-dollared myself to the brink of disaster, I worked my way back to financial solvency by watching all my expenses—especially the little ones. I didn't file for bankruptcy; I paid back every nickel of more than $100,000 of consumer debt (plus all the interest, fees and penalties), and now I live to help others do the same.

The idea that you should live below your means is obvious, isn't it? It's not like this is the first time you've ever heard of the concept. I'm not going to try to convince you that cutting spending isn't hard work; it is! But it's not nearly as hard as living from paycheck to paycheck trying to make ends meet every month.

Every day, thousands of people from around the country read my newspaper column, "Everyday Cheapskate," syndicated by Creators. It's my opportunity to encourage and motivate my readers to manage their money well. I frequently open my mailbag so my clever readers can share their tips for saving time and money. "Everyday Cheapskate" readers love tips, and so do I.

What you have here is a fabulously fun collection of ideas, challenges, suggestions, tips and tricks for ways to do things cheaper, better and faster. Despite a constantly changing world, these ideas stand the test of time.

Some of the best tips you will read have completely unknown origins because they've been passed from generation to generation, and someone along the line sent it my way. They have all been put to the test by yours truly.

I often wonder who benefits more from my column: my readers or me. Writing about how to get out of debt, how to manage an ordinary income in an extraordinary world, and the joy and rewards of living below one's means undoubtedly helps me stay on track. It would be easy to fall back into my old spendthrift ways without the support of my "Everyday Cheapskate" community.

And so, for your enjoyment and reading pleasure, here is a little book packed with fun, unusual and particularly clever ways to save time and money—every day!

—Mary Hunt, Colorado

Gifts, Holidays and Entertaining

Fun (Cheap) Birthday Gift Ideas for Kids

Some time ago, I got a message from Elaine G., who had recently joined a mom's group. With all of her newly minted friendships, she and her child are getting invitations to lots of toddler birthday parties.

Her dilemma took me back to when our boys were small. Birthday parties for all their friends were challenging. That's why Elaine's message grabbed my attention. "Can you help me with ideas for birthday gifts for young children that will score with the kids without breaking our budget?" You bet, Elaine. Try these ideas on for size.

The Story of Me

Give the birthday girl or boy everything they need to write (or draw) the story of their life. For children just learning to read, write or draw, include a list of "prompts" that might include instructing the child to draw a picture of a favorite animal, a place to visit or something that makes them laugh. Package it with a pad or book of drawing paper, markers, crayons and enough prompts to complete all the pages in their book.

Play Kit

Spark the interest and imagination of the birthday child with a custom play kit you put together. "Design" the kit on paper by making a list of contents, and then go "shopping" in your home, garage or attic. Visit thrift stores, garage sales and consignment stores for items that can be laundered and sanitized. Make kits for boys or girls and feature themes such as dress-up, kitchen, handyman, restaurant, doctor, cowboy and entertainer.

Piggy Bank

Start your recipient on the debt-proof road early with a piggy bank. Add a starter fund of coins (or cash, if it's in your budget) to encourage regular deposits that will make the pig noisy when shaken.

Photo Jigsaw Puzzle

Mount an enlarged photo of your child and the birthday boy or girl onto a piece of foam board. Cover the photo with a piece of tracing paper and lightly draw a jigsaw pattern, making the number of pieces appropriate for the recipient's age. Carefully cut through the paper, photo and board along the puzzle lines. Separate the pieces, and place in a gift box.

Bucket of Stuff

Personalize a bucket or container with the birthday child's name, and fill with age-appropriate art and craft supplies like paper, crayons, pencils, glitter, paste, scissors, ruler, tape and a pencil sharpener. A dollar store is a great place to fill a birthday bucket because it's quantity that counts!

Coupon Book

Create a book filled with coupons for play dates with your child and the birthday boy or girl. Include trips to the park, your home, sleepovers, treats, games, crafts and activities.

Jump Rope and Rhymes

This gift is a fun one for elementary-aged kids—and very budget-friendly. Purchase a colorful jump rope, and add the free printable jump rope rhymes you can easily find online with a simple search for "jump rope rhymes."

Coloring Kit

Coloring is popular right now for kids and adults. Putting together a coloring kit makes for an inexpensive gift. Items for the kit might include colored pencils, markers, crayons and one or two coloring books. Purchase them during the fall, when school supplies are on sale for ridiculously awesome prices.

What Teachers Want for Christmas

I've never been a schoolteacher, but I've been a parent. I wish I'd known years ago what I know now about what gifts of thanks teachers really want. I would have skipped all the "Best Teacher in the World" coffee mugs and gone more for the classroom supplies.

Recently, I polled teachers I know. It took a little bit of arm-twisting because every one of them said they appreciate the thought behind every gift they receive, no matter how useless. I did get it out of them. I discovered what teachers really want. So, listen up, and take notes. There may be a quiz.

Make no mistake: Every teacher I spoke with stressed how very grateful teachers are for the thoughts behind all of the stuff they get during the year, the end of the year and the holidays between. But the stuff itself? Not so much. What would you do with 27 random coffee mugs or 16 bottles of aftershave?

General Guidelines

Don't spend a lot on a teacher gift. Keep it reasonable. Parents who go overboard make teachers feel uneasy and awkward.

If you can't afford a gift, don't worry. Show your appreciation by volunteering in the classroom. Teachers don't generally keep score. But they do remember and appreciate classroom volunteers.

Check to see if your school displays teacher "wish lists." That can be very helpful.

If you have time, get a group of parents together to go in on a group gift card or special item for the classroom.

What Teachers Don't Want

Knickknacks. I'm talking cute, goofy, endearing, musical, bric-a-brac, tchotchkes—anything meant to be displayed that collects dust.

Coffee mugs. Every teacher has received dozens already, and even if it is filled with hot chocolate mix or jelly beans—just, no.

Food. This is tricky, and not all teachers were as adamant as some I spoke with. Generally, most teachers don't want the temptation of so many sweets. They get plenty. Others were honest that homemade items leave them uneasy as to the contents, origin and preparation. Sadly, most will simply be tossed out.

Candles. If your teacher has been teaching for anytime at all, he or she has more candles than you can imagine—in every shape, color and scent. Cupboards full of candles.

Jewelry. Especially holiday-themed earrings, bracelets and so on. The teacher will feel obligated to wear it around the student just to be kind, but that's about it.

Lotions and potions. Again, a touchy subject. Lotions, creams, aftershave, cologne, perfume—it's all about personal preference, and unless you have some kind of inside track with the teacher's true desires and personal preferences, skip it.

What Teachers Really Want

Gift cards. But not just any card. Amazon and Starbucks are the most desired, and in any amount. Your $5 Amazon or Starbucks card combined with cards from lots of students will be much appreciated and used. Also mentioned: Nordstrom, Macy's, Staples and Target.

Things for the classroom. Teachers often end up spending money out of their own pockets for supplies. They will be so happy if you help ease the load with a gift. Consider games, books, puzzles, stickers, markers, Post-it notes, dry-erase markers, a ream of copy paper, colored pencils, crayons and so on. It's not difficult to come up with a gift that matches the needs of the classroom.

Movie tickets. The teachers I talked to all agreed that they love having a stash of movie tickets. You can purchase tickets for local theaters at a tremendous discount at Costco—and they never expire.

Thank-you notes. A handwritten note from you and/or your child is something teachers really appreciate. And as you thank the teacher, be specific. Teachers love to know they are making a positive difference in how your child's future is being molded. A note can be a gift all on its own or a nice addition to any of the gifts above.

I know of one teacher who has kept every note and letter

from kids and parents over a very long teaching career. He says this collection is one of his most treasured possessions and one that he goes back to and reads from often.

Thank-You Notes Never Out of Style

Today's column was prompted by a young man, age 10, who asked me recently, "Do I have to send a thank-you note when someone gives me a gift?"

In these high-tech times, when text messaging and email are the preferred methods of written communication, my answer, in a word, was yes. It's right; it's proper; it's good for you. We may be frugal, but we've got class.

It is neither difficult nor time-consuming to write a simple, heartfelt note of thanks in response to a gift or other act of kindness. Here are the elements of a well-written thank-you note:

Greeting

Keep it simple. "Dear Aunt Mary..." works well. Or use another salutation that would roll easily off your tongue, like "Hi," or "Greetings."

Express Gratitude

State your thanks, and identify the specific gift. "Thank you so much for the video game. It's a perfect addition to my Nintendo Switch collection." Or, "Thank you for the sweater, which is the exact color I would have chosen." The only exception to the specific reference is if the gift was money. In that case do not say, "Thank you for the $100." Say simply, "Thank you for the generous gift, which is greatly appreciated." However, in the event that Aunt Mary actually took the time to create a clever presentation, it would be perfectly acceptable to say, "Your generosity is exceeded only by your clever ability to fold money into a beautiful swan." (Note: There are times when mention of the specific amount may be appropriate, as in the receipt of a donation or charitable contribution.)

Discuss Use

A simple sentence that indicates how you will use the gift comes next. "I know I will get plenty of use from this sweater during my semester abroad in Antarctica." Or "It is my all-time favorite game so you can be sure that I will think of you often." Or "It will be spent well to update my shoe collection."

Mention the Past; Refer to the Future

Possibly the most important part of your message is a reference to how this person fits into your life. Something like, "I remember fondly snow tubing with you on the hill behind the barn, and I look forward to seeing you soon." Or, "You are in my thoughts, and I hope to see you soon."

Revisit Gratitude

As you close your note, state again your gratitude. "Thanks again for your gift," is an appropriate way to close your note.

Regards

Wrap things up with a gentle close and your name. "Fondly, Joe" or "Love, Laura" are excellent choices.

There. Seal it up, and get it into the mail. Even if you are the only person you know sending thank-you notes, don't let that deter you. You've demonstrated gracious living at a time when most are too busy to be bothered.

As an added bonus—but certainly not offered as an incentive to do the right thing—thank-you notes have been known to encourage repeat performances, as well as improve the frequency and quality of future gifts.

Don't Go Broke for the Wedding Gift

While tying the knot is getting more expensive for the bride and groom, attending a wedding is becoming costlier, too. Some surveys reveal the average guest will spend $673 this year to attend a single wedding—including but not limited to travel, accommodations and attire.

How Much Should I Spend on a Gift?

I'm not here to tell you what to spend on a gift, but I can offer you a sigh of relief with this: Experts agree you can forget the antiquated notion that you must spend an amount equal to the cost per plate at the reception. A wedding is not a fundraiser. You are not obligated to pony up with a gift that reimburses the cost of your attendance.

Instead, you should come up with a dollar amount that makes sense for you. Never spend more than you can afford on a wedding gift. Going into debt to buy a gift is never a good idea, even if you're sure you can pay it off next month.

Is Cash Acceptable as a Wedding Gift?

While experts pretty much agree it is gauche for a couple to ask for money instead of a wedding gift, it is completely acceptable to give money. Tuck a check or cash inside an envelope with a personal message, or contribute to the couple's online cash registry. If using an envelope, get that to the couple ahead of time, or place it in a receptacle provided for cards at the reception.

How Much Time Do I Have to Give a Wedding Gift?

Traditional wedding etiquette, which still offers you a break on timing, says you have up to a year following the wedding to purchase and send a wedding present.

Compare Prices on Registry Items

It's wise to reference a registry to see what the couple wants, but it's even smarter to compare prices among stores. Retailers like Costco and Overstock sell popular registry brands for less than most high-end stores. In that case, send it to the couple early so yours is not the duplicate.

Use Discount Gift Cards

If you're planning to give a gift card, or you're buying an item off a couple's registry, save money by purchasing discount gift cards from Raise.com. The site offers gift cards for less than face value—for example, a $100 Macy's gift card for $80.

Know Where To Find Coupon Codes

Most stores offer coupons these days, you just have to know where to look to find them. By signing up to receive an e-newsletter from Pottery Barn, Williams-Sonoma and countless other online retailers, you'll get a coupon code for 10% off a future order.

Head to a Warehouse Club

Big box stores like Costco and Sam's Club sell popular registry items like blenders, food processors and other household goods for at least 30% less.

Go In on a Big Gift

If the couple registered for an expensive item that is out of range for one person to afford, find a group of friends or relatives to split the cost.

Buy Gift Wrap and Cards at the Dollar Store

While the cost of wrapping the gift and signing the greeting card seems insignificant, you may be tacking on another $20 to an already pricey present. It all adds up! Duck into the dollar store to get these items for a buck each; you'll be amazed at the selection and quality.

Offer Your Services

If money is tight, offer your services instead of a physical gift. Whether it's doing hair and makeup for the bride and her maids, putting your photography skills to work at the ceremony or dogsitting while the couple's away on their honeymoon, your gift is sure to please.

Spread Out Your Purchases

If you recently bought a gift for the bridal shower or booked airfare and a hotel for the wedding, don't feel pressured to purchase a gift right away, especially if funds are limited. The bride and groom would never want you to go into debt to attend their nuptials, so space out your expenses. Simply follow the traditional wedding etiquette rule and send a gift later. Just don't forget!

The Gentle Art of Gift Giving

The simple act of gift giving has become extremely complicated. I blame that on the consumer credit industry. Think about it: You can be completely broke but still spend thousands of dollars on wedding, graduation, birthday and Christmas gifts—and believe it is not only your right to do so but also your obligation to do it. We believe the message that we have to spend a lot for gifts to be socially acceptable.

Gift giving is a custom that has pretty much run amok. But it doesn't have to be that way. We can choose to make wise and reasonable decisions about the gifts we give.

How many of you cannot recall the special-occasion gifts you gave last year? How about the gifts you received? Come on, let's see those hands. OK, that's just about everybody.

It's not because we're total ingrates that we have trouble remembering the gifts we gave, or even the ones we received. It's because when it's all over, the gifts pale in comparison to the joy they deliver—the love and best wishes for the special event or the season. That's what we carry with us when we receive a gift.

Gifts Are Messengers

They are tokens of the esteem we hold for people we care about. They deliver our love and our best wishes. Gifts express the fondness we have for another person. Without the care, love or concern, the gift is empty. Giving a gift just so you can mark a name off a list is a hollow effort that is likely to fall flat no matter how much money you spend.

Give Something You Made

Whether it's something from your kitchen, your craft room, your woodworking shop or your computer, there's just nothing like a homemade gift. A plate of cookies, a loaf of bread, note cards—these are just some of the kinds of homemade gifts with universal appeal.

Give the Gift of Compassion

Do you want your gift to say how much you care? Then find a way to show you care about what matters most to that person. Is he or she passionate about medical research? Become a bone marrow donor. An environmentalist? Donate to an organization that reforests and plant a tree in his/her name. Do something that this person will find meaningful, and then do it in their honor. Write a description of your experience, and give it to the person.

Give What You Do Best

Often the most meaningful gifts and most difficult ones to give are those that cost no money at all. A gift from the heart is a gift of time and talent. What do you do well? Cook, clean, babysit, garden, sew, drive, shop? Whatever it is, create a unique gift certificate and make what you do the gift that you give: a weekend of babysitting, a day of housecleaning, six hours of errand running—you get the idea. Hint: Follow up within just a few days to set the exact time your certificate will be redeemed. Your recipient may be too embarrassed to remind you to make good on the gift.

Give It in Writing

Worried that your gifts—homemade or otherwise—are too cheap or not exactly right? All of your doubts will vanish when you include a short note with each one telling the recipients what they mean to you and the value they bring to your life.

The best gift is one that delivers a message of love and joy and remains with the recipient long after it has been consumed, used or put away.

Flavored Vinegars Make Elegant Holiday Gifts

Just as I was wondering what on earth I would do with all of the basil, oregano and chives in my garden, here came a note from Ginny M. of Minnesota: "I love using flavored vinegars. How can I make my own?"

Her note reminded me that herb vinegars are so easy to make, but also that the holidays are not many months away. Flavor-infused vinegars make elegant gifts.

To get started, you'll need fresh herbs (mint, basil, tarragon, dill, oregano and chives) clean glass jars with lids and plain white distilled vinegar. Eventually, you'll also need decorative containers, such as bottles or jars, for your finished vinegar. Empty, cleaned wine bottles make great presentation containers for homemade infused vinegar.

Sterilize all of your glass containers by boiling them with the lids removed for 10 minutes. You want to inhibit the growth of microorganisms that can cloud vinegars.

Herb Vinegar

Wash your fresh herbs well and pat dry. Insert about three sprigs of fresh herbs (or 3 tablespoons dried herbs) for each pint of vinegar into a sterilized glass jar. Pour the vinegar over the herbs, filling the jar. Distilled white and apple cider vinegar are most affordable. White wine vinegar is more expensive, but has a very smooth flavor.

The vinegar may be added either hot (just below the boiling point) or cold. Hot vinegar will produce a stronger flavor; cold vinegar will give a milder result.

Tightly cap the jar. Store your herb vinegar in a cool, dark place for several weeks. Don't store it in the refrigerator. Once the desired flavor is reached, pour the vinegar through a coffee filter into sterilized smaller containers. Add a sprig of fresh herb for visual effect and to identify the flavors. Citrus rind, garlic, peppers or peppercorns can also add unique flavors to herbal vinegars. Experiment by combining flavors such as lemon rind and pepper or basil and garlic. Cover or cork your containers tightly.

Raspberry Vinegar

Combine 1/2 cup sugar with 1 cup fresh raspberries in a non-aluminum saucepan. Heat over medium heat, stirring occasionally until hot but not boiling. Pour into a glass bowl and gradually stir in 1 1/2 cups white vinegar. Stir raspberries into the vinegar. Cover with plastic wrap and let stand in a cool place for about a week. Strain through cheesecloth twice, or once through a coffee filter. Pour into a jar or bottle that has a tight-fitting lid or cork. Store in the refrigerator for up to six months.

Cranberry Vinegar

In a large nonmetal bowl, pour 1 quart of white wine vinegar that has been heated just below the boiling point over 2 cups of fresh cranberries. Let the mixture steep covered on the counter for two to three days. Strain the brightly-colored vinegar through a coffee filter and pour into a decorative glass bottle. Insert a cork or plastic cover. Store in the refrigerator.

As a general rule, plastic lids or corks are best for closing vinegars—not metal, which may rust.

Label your vinegar with the type of base vinegar used, the flavoring ingredient, whether it requires refrigeration, and the date. Suggest as well that it will be best when used within six months as an addition to salad dressings, sauces, meat dishes and cooked vegetables.

Thanks, Ginny. Your question put me into holiday gift preparation mode!

Take the Stress out of Entertaining With a Themed Potluck

Whether you are invited or doing the inviting, throwing a potluck can relieve a lot of stress. When everybody brings something, it takes a great deal of pressure off the host and offers guests the joy of contributing to the occasion.

Hosting Duties

If you're hosting, you need to pick a theme for the menu, like Comfort Food, Winter Warmups or Family Favorites.

For a dozen people, you will need approximately two or three appetizers, two side dishes, bread and butter, two desserts, one salad and one main dish.

Provide the main course—ham, turkey or a hearty casserole, for example.

When selecting your potluck menu, look for recipes and dishes that can be prepared in advance, can be reheated at the destination and offer leeway in serving time.

Assign each guest a dish to bring. You can even provide the exact recipe, if you have a particular menu in mind. This will eliminate the possibility of duplication.

Plan the seating, table settings, fun decorations and background music.

Clear space in the refrigerator for cold dishes, and create a schedule for dishes that will require oven time.

Preheat your oven to 350 degrees F, and then turn it off. As guests arrive with hot dishes, place them in the warm oven.

Gather plenty of utensils and serving dishes. Buy small, disposable containers so guests can take home leftovers.

Food Safety

Don't run the risk of ruining a great potluck.

Discard any leftovers that have been left at room temperature for more than two hours.

Keep hot things hot and cold things well-chilled until serving time.

To prevent the slightest chance of food-safety compromise,

put out small portions of perishable items and replenish as needed. Use a new serving dish, or wash the empty one before refilling.

Guest Duties

If you're a contributing guest, you need to:

Plan to have your food finish cooking just as you're ready to leave home.

Bring your assigned dish table-ready and as close to being ready to eat as possible, including an appropriate serving dish and utensils.

Wrap hot dishes in several layers of foil and a thick towel to prevent heat loss. Pack cold dishes in ice in a cooler.

Consider bringing your assigned dish in a slow cooker. This will relieve the host's oven or stovetop that may be in hot demand.

Arrive on time—not late, not early, unless you've checked with the host.

Alert the host in advance if your dish will require final prep (assembly, heating, baking) at the destination.

Serving the Meal

Buffet style is the easiest way to serve a potluck meal. Place plates at the beginning of the line and silverware and napkins at the end.

Leave room on the buffet table for guests to set plates down in case they need both hands to serve themselves.

There you go—all you need to know to put together a lovely, casual event. Sit back; relax; and enjoy your hard work.

Shopping Tips

The Inside Buzz on Batteries

Little things mean a lot—like the two words "batteries included." Just knowing they're in there somewhere means less hassle and one less thing to buy. But face it. The initial powering-up of a battery-operated device is a minor concern. It's the cost of keeping it going for years to come that should be considered.

The commercials are compelling, but can they be trusted? Does a copper top really make a difference? Is Energizer the heavy artillery of battery power? Is heavy-duty superior to alkaline? Are el-cheapo, generic batteries evidence that you get what you pay for? Is heavy-duty superior to alkaline?

Alkaline Versus Heavy-Duty

Consumers Union, which publishes Consumer Reports Magazine, concluded that when it comes to single-use batteries, the alkaline and lithium varieties are by far the best performers. Even the most expensive heavy-duty battery cannot compete with the cheapest alkaline or lithium.

So, the conclusion is clear: Buy alkaline, which is cheaper than lithium, and buy according to price, not by brand. Go for the store or generic brands, and when you find them on sale, stock up.

Retailers such as Costco, Target and Walmart don't own their own battery factories. They contract with the biggies such as Rayovac, Eveready and Duracell. Private-label batteries are typically the exact same product as the national brands; only the label and the price are different.

Expiration Dates

Alkaline batteries have a life of about five years. However, they lose power slightly when not in use. That is why you should always look for the latest "best if used by" date code.

Storing Batteries

It's not exactly a myth that storing batteries in the refrigerator will preserve their energy, but it's close. Tests indicate chilled batteries have only a slight, if any, increase in life expectancy over batteries stored at room temperature—no more than 10%.

Rechargeable Batteries

Even the best rechargeable NiCad batteries do not perform as long on a single charge as the same number of single-use alkaline. However, for power-hungry items such as CD players, games and other items that get lots of use, rechargeables make a lot of sense because they can be recharged hundreds of times.

Rechargeable NiCads are not recommended for low-drain devices or passive applications such as smoke detectors and alarm clocks.

Rechargeable alkaline batteries, which are less expensive than NiCads, lose significant capacity with each recharge and have a life expectancy of only about 25 recharges.

Safety tip: Experts say we should install fresh batteries in smoke detectors and security systems every six months. But don't throw the old batteries out. They likely have lots of life remaining, especially if they are alkaline, and will work well in your remote control, pager, toys and flashlights.

Disposal

All batteries should be recycled to keep them out of the landfills. Home Depot stores have collection bins. Or check with your county government about other collection facilities in your area.

Things You Can Do Now To Fight Price Inflation

Nearly everything at the store, from beef and cereal to fruit and veggies, costs more than it did a year ago. Inflation is the culprit eating away at your budget.

You may not have noticed yet because it takes a while for these changes to trickle down. But we need to be keenly aware of what's going on to stay ahead of this. We need to know what to do now.

Beat the Shrink

Inflation doesn't always show up in the price of an item. It may appear that nothing has changed, but check the product size. It's a sneaky and common way that retailers hide inflation. They shrink the size of the product but leave the price the same.

Sugar used to come in 5-pound bags. Now that same sugar comes in 4-pound bags with no change in price.

There was a time when coffee came in 1-pound and 3-pound sizes. Have you looked lately? Most brands' pound of coffee is now 12 ounces. A 3-pound container is closer to 30 ounces.

Your best defense to beat the shrink is to start noticing. Look for hidden inflation every time you shop. Know your prices. Check the labels. Compare brands.

Buy in Bulk

Basic pantry staples are much cheaper when purchased in bulk quantities. These are items that store well in a cool, dark pantry for a very long time—rice, beans, flour, oil and so forth.

Roast and Grind

With the price of coffee up more than 25% over the past year, perhaps it's time to get serious about roasting and grinding your own coffee beans.

You'll cut the cost by half or more and enjoy drinking some delicious coffee. I've been home-roasting coffee for more than a decade. Currently, I roast with a Behmor 1600 home coffee roasting machine and import raw green coffee beans from Costa Rica.

The Coffee Bean Corral is an online bulk supplier that has good prices on green coffee beans in bags of 5 to 132 pounds, starting as low as $5.75 per pound. There are lots of online videos to teach you how to home-roast coffee.

Use a Tea Ball

If you're a serious tea drinker and you buy those little boxes of tea bags, you're spending way too much per pound for your tea. Do the math, and try not to choke when you discover how much you are spending per pound.

Here's a novel idea: Get a tea ball, also referred to as a loose tea infuser. Or if you prefer disposable tea bags, you can buy empty tea bags to fill yourself. Now you can purchase fine, fresh loose tea in bulk and slash your per-tea bag cost in ways that will have you singing hallelujah!

Grow a Garden

Wish you could grow an edible garden but don't have the space for it? I've got good news.

You don't need acreage, a big yard or perfect conditions. In fact, you really don't need any yard at all. There are myriad ways you can get started today growing your own food—in a barrel or big pot. On a deck or porch. You can even grow vegetables in a black trash bag! It's easy.

Join Up

Consider joining a local community-supported agriculture, or CSA, program. Or join an online produce supplier such as Misfits Market or Imperfect Foods.

Members of CSAs pay dues, which buy shares of a local farm. These dues go directly to pay for seeds, fertilizer, water, equipment and labor. The harvest is divided between shareholders. Costs to produce can vary widely, depending on location and other factors.

To get started, go to https://www.localharvest.org/, and search their network.

And now for this distressing fact: Almost a third of food grown in the U.S. never gets harvested because it doesn't meet the superficial standards of a traditional grocery store. And yet, there are millions of food-insecure households in the U.S.

Both Misfits Market and Imperfect Foods are committed to fighting food waste by making healthy, quality food more accessible. If you are not offended by misshapen produce, you can save at least 40% by ordering from these companies.

7 Easy Ways to Slash the Cost of Clothing

Clothing is not optional, but spending a lot of money on it is, says author Gregory Karp in his book "Living Rich by Spending Smart: How to Get More of What You Really Want."

So, just off the top of your head, how much would you say that your family spends on clothing in a year? According to the U.S. Consumer Expenditure Survey 2019, a "consumer unit" (people who live and spend money together) spent on average $1,883 a year on apparel and services such as dry cleaning. Wow. That's $157 a month—which is a significant expense in any family's budget.

Karp offers seven easy ways to cut that expense without having to take fashion risks for yourself or send the kids off to school looking odd and frumpy.

No. 1: Do Nothing

Of course, this is my favorite of the seven tips. Maybe that's because I'm naturally lazy, or maybe it's because I, like many, have enough clothes to get by for months. Do with what you have by recognizing the difference between needs and wants.

No. 2: Buy Used

Vintage, consignment and thrift stores are growing by leaps and bounds, offering name-brand used clothes. If you're creeped out by the thought of buying secondhand, take a tour of a few stores. They're not usually the dark, smelly, chaotic places you remember as a kid. Most these days are just as lovely as regular retail stores. And if you're really uncomfortable buying used clothing, here's a tip from Karp: Take baby steps by buying just one time. You could try purchasing something inexpensive at a high-end consignment store.

No. 3: Use Garage Sales Wisely

Garage sales can be a great source for clothes for kids and babies. They're probably not so useful for adults, though, for the simple reason that you won't find enough inventory to offer a good selection of sizes, styles and colors.

No. 4: Strategize

Most of us have wardrobes jammed haphazardly with so

many clothes, it's nearly impossible to know what we have. So, we just keep buying more. Instead, organize your closet, and take inventory of what you have. And, says Karp, buy for the size you are now, not the size you someday hope to be.

No. 5: Simplify

Buy classic styles that will look good for years. Assemble a base of neutral colors—such as black, khaki and navy—that can mix and match to create a number of outfits. Ditto for shoes.

No. 6: Save On Retail

If you won't buy secondhand, Karp recommends going to your favorite store's website to check its sales every week. Sign up for that store's email newsletters to receive coupons and notice of coming sales.

No. 7: Pay Attention to Maintenance

Read the tags before you buy. If a garment must be dry-cleaned, that is going to add to its cost tremendously over its useful life. Also, steer clear of fabrics that tend to pill or wear too fast. Make sure you use the proper temperatures for washing and drying your clothes. A great tip: Put your clothes in the dryer for just a few minutes, and then hang them to dry. You'll save on energy costs and extend the life of your clothes as well.

Highly Effective Ways to Chop the Soaring Cost of Groceries

Perhaps you've noticed the cost of nearly everything is going up. The Bureau of Labor Statistics Consumer Price Index, the agency that calculates the U.S. inflation rate, is predicting a very high inflation rate for 2021. Our annual inflation rate at the end of May was running at 5%. That is the highest rate since 1981, when the average for that year was 10.3%.

Here's the deal: We can either stick our heads in the sand and pretend that nothing has changed, or we can get smart and fight back.

Which brings me to the point of this column: To revisit the most effective ways to cut the cost of groceries and then make sure we are practicing them with determination and vengeance.

Shop the Sales

Check grocery ads for specials, then base your week's meals on what's on sale. The closer you can stick to buying only what's on sale, the more you'll cut your costs.

Don't Shop Hungry

You will be compelled to buy everything in sight regardless of what's on your list if you arrive at the store hungry. Tip: If you can't avoid it, head to the bakery and pick up a cookie, or grab a protein bar on your way in. That will be enough to silence your hunger and clear your mind.

Leave the Kids at Home

You will stick to your shopping list and complete your mission with less frustration and stress if you fly solo.

Cook from Scratch

Cooking and baking using raw ingredients rather than those that are highly processed or prepared is one of the most effective ways to slash food costs.

Pinch of Salt

Sounds weird, I know but this really works: Add a pinch of table salt to a new container of milk when you first open it. Shake well to mix. Because salt retards the growth of bacteria that makes milk turn sour, just a pinch of salt will increase the useful life of milk by days, even weeks. Don't worry, such a small amount will not alter the taste or be detectable in any way.

Stretch Concentrated Fruit Juice

Always add one can of water more than the instructions state. You will be pleasantly surprised when you detect little difference, if any.

Drink Water

Your doctor will love you, and so will your food bill, as you replace carbonated sugary beverages with inexpensive water. Keep a pitcher of chilled water in the fridge. Rave about its wonderful qualities to your young children. They'll think it's a treat if you are convincing enough.

Eliminate Choices at Meals

Find yourself making a variety of menus to please everyone at the table? It might be time to move to a single menu. Let the family know that from now on there will be only two choices: take it or leave it.

Consider Generic and Store Brands

Some generic items are awful and others are exactly the same product as the name brand. Do some experimenting, especially if your store offers "satisfaction guaranteed!" If you don't like it, get a refund or an exchange.

Shop the Perimeter of the Store

This is where you will typically find the produce, meat and dairy. The center aisles are the prepackaged and preprocessed high-priced items, aka the danger zone.

Keep a Price Book

Start keeping a notebook that lists the prices of regularly purchased items at various stores. Keep it with you so that as you see specials or ads, you'll be able to determine whether it is really a bargain or not.

Shop Midweek

On Wednesdays, most supermarkets reduce prices on food that is about to expire, according to several studies. This is also the day that the majority of stores start their new sales.

Creative Procrastination

Even if you think you must get to the supermarket because there's nothing to eat in the house, wait. Hold up. Pretend you're stranded on an island with truly nothing to eat but what you have in the pantry, refrigerator and freezer. Chances are good you'll come up with something, thereby putting more time between shopping trips.

10 Practical Ways to Stretch Your Food Budget

If soaring food prices are getting you down, help is on the way! Here are some basic saving strategies, practical solutions and novel ideas to stretch your food budget and make your life easier.

Granted, one of these strategies on its own is not likely to make a huge difference in your bottom line. But lots of small strategies working together—that's the way to see huge results.

Grate Savings

You pay a lot to have someone else grate your cheese for you. It's at least twice the price of buying cheese by the block. Currently, at my supermarket, cheese in blocks runs from about $2 to $2.50 a pound for the store brand to about $5 a pound or more for name brands. The very same cheeses pre-grated run almost exactly double across the board, $4 to $10 a pound. Here's the tip: Grate it yourself. It will stay fresher, and you'll save money, too.

Breakfast for Dinner

Once a week or so, consider having breakfast for dinner. Kids love this, and so will your food budget. A meal of eggs, pancakes or waffles, and juice is nutritious, meatless and super cheap. Get creative with leftovers, and watch how far you can stretch your food dollars. Those leftover baked potatoes from last night's dinner will make fabulous hash browns or fried potatoes to go with scrambled eggs.

Eat the Sales

Plan your meals around what's on sale, and you'll chop your food costs by up to 50% or more. And when you can, load up on super sale items to last until the next time they go on sale. Nearly every grocery store or supermarket publishes their weekly sales online. What a handy way to help with meal planning.

Veggie Bouquet

Store asparagus in the fridge in a glass of water (like cut flowers in a vase). It will stay fresh for a couple of weeks. This trick works with celery, too. Discover every possible way you can stop throwing away precious food dollars in the form of rotten produce.

Longer-Lasting Tomatoes

Store tomatoes stem-side down to keep them from spoiling as quickly. This prevents air from entering and moisture from exiting the scar where the tomato was once attached to the vine. Storing them at room temperature rather than in the fridge also makes tomatoes last longer.

Beef in Bulk

Buying the "family size" package of ground beef will chop the cost per pound significantly! But if you use it up faster just because you have more, there go the savings. When you get home, you need a reliable way to divide the meat into usable portions.

Do-It-Yourself Buttermilk

To make buttermilk when there's none of the real stuff in the fridge, add a tablespoon of vinegar or lemon juice to regular milk. The mixture won't get as thick and creamy as buttermilk, but it will help create fluffy pancakes and quick bread just the same. Your recipe will turn out great, and you'll have saved yourself a potentially expensive trip to the market.

Bye, Bugs

To protect dry staples such as flour, meal, grits, pasta and rice from contamination, pop a dry bay leaf or two into the container. This won't affect the taste, but it will prevent pesky bugs from ruining these products.

Weigh Bagged Produce

Use the handy scale in the produce department to weigh pre-weighed bags. For example, if you're buying a 5-pound bag of potatoes, weigh several bags. The bags will vary, and you're sure to find one that's 5 1/2 pounds or heavier for the same price!

Leftover Buffet

Take the remains of the week's meals, and serve them for dinner, buffet style. Need to pad the offerings? Raid the fridge for veggies and dip; make a green salad; toast some crusty bread. Keep this idea handy. You just might decide to make Leftover Night a weekly occurrence!

Confused in the Supermarket

Dear Mary: Can you clarify expiration dates on food products? When it says "sell by 4/01/21," does that mean it has to be used or just sold by that date? Others show a date of, say, "2/01/23" on canned or packaged goods. Does that mean you need to use it by this date, or what? Some canned or packaged products don't seem to have any date that I can find. Why is that? I'm so confused!—Bobbye

Dear Bobbye: Great question! The answer, which I can promise you will be much longer than your question, may surprise you.

While most food processors date and code their products, the Food and Drug Administration mandates dating ONLY on infant formula and baby food. Everything else is voluntary. Still, the food industry generally follows certain guidelines suggested by the FDA.

Phrases like "best before," "better if used before" or "best if used by" tell you how long the product will retain its best flavor and highest quality. They are found on products like baked goods, cereals, snacks and some canned foods. The food is still safe to eat after this date, but it may have changed in taste and or texture.

The "sell by" date is usually found on highly perishable foods such as meat, milk and bread. This date guides the rotation of shelf stock and allows time for the product to be stored and used at home. The product is still safe and wholesome past this date. For example, milk will usually be good for at least a week beyond its "sell by" date, if properly refrigerated. Meat that has arrived at its "sell by" date should be either consumed or frozen within 24 hours. You can also extend the useful life of milk and baked goods by freezing within a day or so of the "sell by" date.

"Expiration," "use by" or "use before" are phrases that appear on yogurt, eggs and other foods that require refrigeration. Other dating terms are guidelines, but this one means what it says. If you haven't used the product by this date, toss it out.

"Guaranteed fresh." This date is often used for perishable

baked goods. Beyond this date, freshness is no longer guaranteed, although the product may still be edible.

Some products bear a "pack date," indicating when it was packaged, although this date is often encrypted so that only manufacturers, wholesalers and retailers can read it. The pack date on some products, such as eggs, is shown by numbers 1 through 365; Jan. 1 is no. 1, and Dec. 31 is no. 365. In other coding, letters A through M (omitting the letter I) are often assigned to the months, with A being January and M being December, plus a numeric day either preceded or followed by the numeric year.

The point in all of this is that the fresher your food, the better it is. And processors want to assure customers that their products will remain at peak quality for certain periods of time.

Pro tip: In a properly stocked store, the freshest items will be at the back of the shelf or underneath older items.

Home Care: Cleaning, Laundry & Organization

Absolutely the Best Homemade Laundry Stain Remover

I'm excited to tell you how to make a fabulous, if not magical, do-it-yourself homemade stain remover. This stain remover recipe is so easy and cheap to make. And wow, does it perform!

Just let me be clear at the get-go: While this stain remover works super well on fabric, upholstery and carpet in the house and car, it must be rinsed well or laundered once that stain disappears. Got it? OK, let's get right to it.

You will need:

Fresh hydrogen peroxide
Blue Dawn dishwashing liquid
Spray bottle, any size
Funnel (optional)

Into a small bottle, using a funnel if desired, pour 1 part Blue Dawn and 2 parts fresh hydrogen peroxide, i.e., 1 cup Blue Dawn and 2 cups hydrogen peroxide or 1/4 cup Blue Dawn and 1/2 cup hydrogen peroxide. You can use any size bottle to make up any amount of laundry stain remover you need or want!

To use: Shake bottle to mix. Apply to stain.

Wait a few minutes. Don't be surprised when that stain disappears all by itself! If it doesn't, rub the stain with a brush or clean white cloth (you don't want to transfer color from a cleaning cloth to the stained item).

Launder the item as usual. If treating carpet or upholstery, rinse and blot with clear water, keeping in mind that you've just sprayed full-strength dishwashing detergent on that sofa, chair or carpet. It needs to be completely removed.

This DIY laundry stain remover is a miracle worker all around the house. I use it on kitchen and bath linens, clothes, carpet, rugs, white sofas and dining room chairs. It tackles red wine stains, organic stains such as blood and grass, pet stains and baby stains. You can use this on colored items as well as whites (although test it first in an inconspicuous place).

FAQs

Q: Do I have to use Blue Dawn, or can I substitute something else?

A: You can substitute any kind of liquid dishwashing soap, although I wouldn't unless it's an emergency. That's because Blue Dawn contains specific surfactants that are far more effective on grease and oil than any other product in its class. And if you use Blue Dawn Ultra, your results will be even more spectacular because the Ultra version contains enzymes. That makes it really effective on proteins, which most household stains contain.

Q: Why do you specify "fresh" hydrogen peroxide?

A: Hydrogen peroxide dissipates and loses its effectiveness in the presence of light—both sunlight and household light. If you use an old bottle of hydrogen peroxide in this recipe that you've had sitting on the shelf for years, you might as well just use water. It's worn out and lost its spunk. Keeping your bottle of homemade stain remover in an amber bottle will help to protect it from light. Putting the bottle in a dark cupboard will protect it even further. The rule of thumb is this: Once opened, keep hydrogen peroxide tightly sealed in a dark place, and use it within six months.

Ways to Use Windex That Have Nothing to Do With Windows

Recently, while digging out, cleaning up and reorganizing our storage room, I discovered a half-full jug of Windex. I have to admit that for a few moments, it was like Christmas, and not because I was itching to clean windows. It's because I know lots of situations where Windex comes to the rescue to make life easier!

What's In It?

Windex now comes in at least 12 varieties of cleaners, including Windex with ammonia, Windex with vinegar, a "crystal rain" scented option and even Windex Electronics Screen Wipes. But the original version remains the most popular and readily available. And, by the way, Windex Advanced has been discontinued. Who knows? Maybe it's a collector's item!

According to SC Johnson, the original-formula Windex contains cleaning agents, wetting agents, fragrance and color. This makes it ideal for more than just cleaning glass and mirrors:

Laundry Stains

Windex makes for a super effective stain remover on nonsilk washable fabrics—especially on difficult red stains such as red wine, tomato sauce and ketchup. Spray the stain liberally with Windex; allow it to soak in and work for 20 minutes or so; and then rinse it out with cold water. Launder as usual. Caution: Stick with the clear, colorless version of Windex when using it to remove stains from white or light items.

Bug Spray

Hit those ants and other creepy-crawlies with a mist of Windex and watch them curl up and die. Many readers have reported this works really well, but once cleaned up, it will not prevent the bugs from coming back. To do that, spray the cleaned-up area with a light mist of white vinegar to create a more lasting barrier.

Kitchen Degreaser

Windex works as a degreaser for cooktops, range hoods, fans, light fixtures and other areas that attract grease and grime.

Spray the area with Windex and allow it to sit for a few minutes, then wipe clean. Rinse well if using near food preparation areas.

Windex is great on countertops, too, including quartz, granite, marble, laminate and tile. Just make sure that if you're cleaning natural stone counters that have a sealant, such as granite, marble or quartzite, you're using a Windex version that is free of ammonia and vinegar.

Microfiber Upholstery

Microfiber, a synthetic fabric, has become a popular textile for upholstered furniture, because it is super durable and inexpensive. Microfiber is beautiful, too, but stains easily and can be super challenging to clean. Even water can leave an ugly spot on microfiber. Windex to the rescue! Spritz the area lightly with Windex. Quickly, before it can soak in, use a soft bristle brush or clean white terrycloth to lightly scrub and whisk away the stain. Be careful to work in just one direction. A difficult stain might require a second treatment.

Stainless Steel

When cleaning a window with Windex, you want to be able to see your reflection looking back at you. Well, the same goes for stainless steel surfaces.

Stuck Rings

Need help getting a ring off after it has been on your finger for a long time? Try putting on a few drops of Windex, and it will pop right off.

Jewelry Cleaner

Soak gold, silver, diamonds, rubies, emeralds and other pieces of fine jewelry for a few minutes in a small container filled with Windex. Brush them with a soft, old toothbrush, and then rinse well in clear water. Buff dry and look at that sparkle! Caution: Never use Windex on soft stones such as opals or costume jewelry.

Sink and Faucets

Clean your stainless steel sink and faucet with soap and water, and then dry with a clean microfiber cloth. Next, spray the sink and faucet with Windex, and wipe dry for super shiny results.

Stubborn Zippers

This hack will make everyone's life a little better. Have you ever had to throw out a jacket or pair of pants because of a stuck zipper? Use Windex to free the problematic zipper. What a slick idea.

Simple Ways to Unclog a Drain Without Toxic Chemicals

A plugged-up sink, shower or tub drain sends most people running for either a bottle of caustic drain cleaner or a plumber's phone number. But wait: Unclogging a drain might be a job you could successfully do yourself without chemicals or a big bill.

Assess the Situation

Turn on taps to allow water down other drains in the house. If everything else is flowing freely, you can be fairly certain you have a localized clog, and it's probably near that clogged drain's opening.

If the problem involves other drains, you could have a bigger problem that might require a professional. Assuming it's only the one drain, let's move on.

Boiling Water

Get a large pot and boil up as much water as it will hold. However, if you are dealing with a very old porcelain sink and/or PVC pipes, then there's a slight chance that boiling water could cause damage. In that case, fill the pot with your very hottest tap water.

Now, carefully and slowly, pour the boiling or hot water down the drain in two to three stages so that the water can work for a few minutes in between each pour. This is the easiest and quickest way to unclog a drain, if it works—and it usually does, with a satisfying swoosh.

Blue Dawn

Pour 1/2 cup of Blue Dawn detergent (for the best result, do not use substitutes) into the drain. For tough clogs, use a full cup.

While that sits, bring about 4 cups of water to a boil. Pour this into the drain slowly but steadily to avoid getting burned by splashing water. Next, run water to check how freely it flows through the drain.

If the clog remains or the drain is still slow-running even though it seems to be clearing, repeat the boiling water step until the drain runs free.

Baking Soda and Vinegar

Measure out 1/3 cup of baking soda, and get as much of it down the drain as you can. Follow with 1/3 cup of white vinegar. It will fizz up and make quite a show. Allow it to sit for at least an hour, or overnight if at all possible. In the morning, follow with a quart or two of boiling water. You will be tempted to overdo it with the baking soda and vinegar. Don't.

Reach In

Remove the strainer that is part of the drain plug, and then reach into the drain with your fingers (latex gloves would be a good idea here), and pull out any solids. As gross as this might be, it is often all that's needed to clear a slow-moving or clogged drain.

Wet/Dry Vacuum

If you have a wet/dry vacuum, it just might help you to clear the drain without having to get your hands dirty. First, set it to wet so it vacuums liquids. Cover or close the drain's vent. Then, make the tightest seal you can with the hose end of the vacuum over the drain: Get creative with duct tape or the like. With the vacuum set to its most powerful setting, it can be powerful enough to pull that clog right out of the drain. Don't forget to clean the vacuum tank!

No Guarantees

While I offer no guarantees, because not all clogged drains are created equal, attempting to clear a clogged drain yourself first—before spending money or just living with it until you have a major disaster—is certainly worth a shot.

I can't tell you the number of times I've successfully cleared a stubborn clogged drain—especially in a bathroom sink or shower—with this method. Use a drain-cleaning tool such as a Zip-It first for best results. Seriously awesome!

How to Wash White Laundry to Keep It Looking Brilliant

In the same way there are rules in life for things like how to drive a car, how to cook a meal or how to manage your money, there are a few simple rules for how to wash white clothes to keep them looking brilliant and clean. And if they happen to get a bit dull, gray or yellowed, there are rules for how to restore the brightness of washable white clothing, too.

Separate

Sort dirty laundry carefully. Never allow items of color—any color, no matter how pale—to sneak into a load of white laundry. Washing white clothes separately prevents the dye from colored items from bleeding and transferring to white things. Even though the effect may not be noticeable at first, this is how white things begin their journey to become dull and dingy eventually.

Treat Stains

Make sure you pre-treat all stains on white clothes before putting them into the washer. This is your window of opportunity to make sure they will be completely removed—before they hit the washer and dryer.

Want to know the best stain remover? It's there under your kitchen sink: Blue Dawn Ultra dishwashing liquid. Fill a squeeze bottle, and keep it in the laundry room. When you see a stain, hit it with a bit of full-strength Blue Dawn Ultra, and then launder as usual. It works like magic on most stains on both white and colored items. Just make sure you keep the whites and colors in separate loads!

Avoid Overcrowding

White things need their space to get really clean and white. Suppose the washer is packed to capacity. That leaves precious little room between these items for the water to move powerfully enough to flush away the soil that the detergent will have loosened. When left to dry on fabric, that left-in residue will leave those items looking dull and, eventually, gray.

Overcrowding is not good for any laundry loads, but it's

especially troublesome for white clothes.

More Is Not Better

Whether yours is an older top-loading machine that uses a lot of water or a front-loader that uses what seems like hardly any, chances are good you're using way too much detergent. It is difficult to imagine, perhaps, but you should measure by tablespoons, not cups, with most machines. Experiment to find the right amount for your machine, or follow the label instructions (warily), and then carefully measure for each load.

Detergent that doesn't get rinsed away thoroughly gets stuck between the fibers of your white towels and sheets and will make them feel rough and scratchy, not soft and fluffy—and eventually dingy gray.

Hot, Hot, Hot

Use hot water in the wash cycle for white items (or the warmest recommended for the fabric) and cold water for the rinse cycle(s). This helps to remove body oils and grime that can leave fabric looking dingy and gives the dirty detergent the best opportunity to be rinsed away completely.

Rinse With Vinegar

Forget commercial fabric softeners, which can leave residue on fabrics that can be harmful to our health and are not good for the washer and dryer, either. Instead, add one cup of distilled white vinegar to the rinse cycle to ensure that all the detergent is stripped away from fabrics.

Double-Check for Stains

Once white items come out of the washer, check again to make sure all stains are gone. If not, re-treat and re-launder. If a stained item goes through the dryer, you've just guaranteed it will be much more difficult to remove, if you manage to remove it at all. Heat treating does that.

Full Sun or Low Heat

If you have the opportunity and the right conditions where you live, hanging your white items out on a line or dryer rack in full sun is ideal. The ultraviolet rays from the sun will sanitize, freshen and whiten them!

If sun is not possible, dry whites on a low heat setting in the clothes dryer. This will take a bit longer, but your items will last longer, and any stains, dinginess or grayish tinge will be much easier to reverse. Overdrying can also cause stains you can't see to turn yellow.

9 Favorite Cleaning Formulas

The next time you need cleaning supplies, take a trip to your pantry, not the store. You already have the ordinary basic household items required to mix up every type of cleaner you need to keep the place sparkling clean and germ-free. Recipes? You need recipes? Well, this must be your lucky day because I've got recipes!

All-Purpose Liquid Cleaner

Mix 1/2 cup of white vinegar, 1 cup of plain household ammonia and 1/4 cup of baking soda with 1 gallon of warm water. Dispense in a spray bottle, and use as you would a commercial brand such as Formula 409.

Window, Glass and Mirror Cleaner

In a spray bottle, mix together 2 cups of isopropyl rubbing alcohol, 2 teaspoons of liquid dishwashing detergent and 2 cups water.

Floor Cleaner (For Ceramic and Vinyl Floors)

Mix together 1 cup of white vinegar and 1 gallon of hot water. Mop ceramic tile and all types of vinyl floors with this solution; no need to rinse. Caution: Never use vinegar on hardwood, granite or natural stone products. Over time, it will eat away the sealer and finish.

Wood Floor Cleaner

Mix together 2 quarts of boiling water, and steep two regular tea bags in it. Let the water cool to room temperature. Remove bags. Use a well-wrung cloth mop or sponge mop (make sure it is just barely damp) to wipe the floor. The tannic acid in tea is great for the wood and leaves a beautiful shine.

Heavy-Duty Floor Cleaner

Mix together 3/4 cup of plain household ammonia and 1 gallon of warm water. Use on heavily soiled nonwood floors. No need to rinse.

Tub Cleaner

Pour 1/2 cup of Dawn dishwashing liquid in a spray bottle. Fill the rest of the bottle with vinegar. Spray on tub and enclosures, and scrub. Or, for super challenging situations, allow it to set for a few hours, and then scrub as required. Rinse well. It cleans better than any commercial product, even for the most difficult tub, shower and enclosure challenges.

Furniture Polish

Combine 2 parts olive (or vegetable) oil and 1 part lemon juice (or white vinegar) in a glass jar. Seal tightly. Shake well before using sparingly, applying a thin coat with a soft cloth and buffing well.

Glass Carafe Cleaner

Pour 1 cup of crushed ice into that glass coffee pot (put ice cubes in a plastic bag first, and whack them on the floor or other hard surface). Add 2 tablespoons of table salt. Hold the carafe by the handle, and swirl it around vigorously until you see all the burnt-on coffee and various stains come off. Empty, and rinse thoroughly. This method turns even the grungiest pot sparkling clean. It gives you a little exercise, too.

Jewelry Cleaner

Make a 50-50 mixture of household ammonia and water. Soak jewelry, and then brush and rinse completely. Caution: Do not use this on jewelry that contains opals, pearls or any other soft stone.

Caution: While none of these formulas includes liquid chlorine bleach, if you come up with some of your own formulas, never mix chlorine bleach with any other product. You could create deadly chlorine gas. Always label the products you create. Keep them tightly covered and out of the reach of children and pets.

And one more thing: Don't forget to keep track of all the money you're not spending on pricey commercial cleaning products. It's going to be a lot!

Baby Steps Lead From Clutter to Calm

Recently, I read about a couple who live in Oklahoma City. They don't have a lot of clutter in their house, but they do find it impossible to part with their children's things. The guest cottage behind their house is nearly filled with old toys, outgrown clothes, years of kids' artwork, school papers, trophies, sports paraphernalia, baby beds, bassinets and a rocking horse. Seems they can't bring themselves to clean it out or part with all of these things for fear their now-grown children will think they don't love them.

I know the feeling, and I don't think it's that unusual. But most of us don't have a guest house to stash and hide all the clutter. Thankfully, it is possible to deal with clutter in realistic and reasoned ways so that it doesn't turn into chaos.

Marla Cilley, known to many as the FlyLady and author of the fabulous book, *Sink Reflections*, says CHAOS is an acronym for "Can't Have Anyone Over Syndrome."

The good news is that clutter does not have to control our homes and our lives. It requires only a modicum of determination to take that first baby step toward conquering stuff. Then another and another all the way to peace and serenity.

Front Entry

It's natural to walk into the house and start dumping small things like keys, glasses and mail on the first flat surface you see. "When things get strewn all over, it's because they don't have a clear or intuitive place to go," says professional organizer Shira Gill. Here's a quick and easy way to turn entry chaos into calm: Invest in a storage bench, attractive wall hooks and a catchall tray. Now everything from shoes to keys and phone has a place.

Focus on a Single Location

It's a big fail just waiting to happen when we attempt to declutter an entire room or the whole house in a single weekend. Instead, think small. Focus on a single location like the medicine cabinet, closet or drawer. Remove everything from that space—every single thing. Clean the space thoroughly. Now, evaluate and edit. Once you have culled the things you don't use or don't love, return only the items that belong in this space—things you use regularly or that bring beauty to your life. Drawer dividers or shallow bins are so helpful to keep things organized.

Consider Decanters

It's not at all unusual for the areas we do laundry to turn into disaster zones. It's just the laundry room, right? Imagine walking into that area and feeling at peace because it is so attractive and inviting! Decanters are one solution. Store powdered detergents in clear jars with scoops to make it easy to use and to see when you're running low. Pour stain removers and liquid soap can into olive oil jars with spouts for spill-proof pouring. Add simple labels. See how pretty that looks? Useful, too.

Take Photos

All of those things that you can't part with because they hold such meaning and memory? Take a picture of each one. Take several. Zoom in, pan out. Do a panorama view if you want. Now the memories are preserved in a way you can really enjoy them. And you can part with the actual items, guilt-free.

Stash the Cash

I have a feeling our Oklahoma City friends are sitting on a pile of money. That rocking horse alone could bring a few bucks at a garage sale or advertised on CraigsList. Who knows what other treasures are rotting away out there—things that could be turned into money that would fit nicely in a savings account.

Read this Book

Honestly, I cannot give you a better piece of advice than to read FlyLady's book, *Sink Reflections*, by Marla Cilley available at Amazon and wherever fine books are sold. You'll laugh. You might cry. But for sure you will know what to do, starting right now. Marla is a reformed clutter bug and knows what she's talking about. She could motivate our friends in Oklahoma City to get that guest cottage cleaned out—and in a loving, compelling way that would allow them to retain all of the memories, assure their children of their love and end up with a place for guests to rest, relax and enjoy themselves.

Just because you can't imagine changing your life from chaos to calm in a single day doesn't mean you shouldn't get started. According to Cilley, "Things done imperfectly still bless our lives." And isn't that great news.

Replace or Repair?

You're worried the washing machine may be on its last spin cycle. It makes a horrible screeching sound and needs a lot of coaxing to make it all the way through a full cycle. Should you spend $319 to fix this inefficient appliance or replace it with a $999 new model that will use less electricity and water?

Deciding whether to repair or replace your broken appliance—especially when trying to save money in the long run—can be challenging.

Consider these basic guidelines, based on costs and advantages of both options, to help you decide.

If You Cannot Pay Cash for the New Replacement

You should get it repaired to buy yourself time to save up for the replacement. Even if the repairs will only keep this appliance going for a year or two, you're far better off repairing and then saving for a new machine than paying double-digit interest for the next three to five years.

If You Have Some Cash but Not Enough

Consider replacing your clunker with an older-model, lightly used, high-quality machine. Check sites like Craigslist for well-cared-for, used appliances. Spread the word to friends and neighbors. People are constantly relocating—which means needing to sell perfectly lovely, near-new appliances.

If the Appliance Is Eight or More Years Old

Once an appliance becomes elderly, it usually makes sense to buy a new one. However, if you have a high-end, older appliance, you may want to repair it.

If Repairs Are Really Expensive

If the repair bill is more than half the price of a new product, you should consider buying new rather than repairing it. But again, the deciding factor will be whether or not you will have to go into debt to buy new.

If the Appliance Is Under Warranty

Even if repairs will be only partially covered by a warranty or service contract, repairing is the way to go. If it's under warranty, call a factory-authorized repair shop. If not, an independent contractor is likely to offer better service at a lower cost.

The costs for diagnosing problems and making repairs on home appliances have gone up considerably in the last few years. This has made replacements with new models more common.

A Word to the Wise

Home appliances have intentional obsolescence. By design, life expectancy has gone down slowly over the years. Take refrigerators, for example. They used to last for 30 years or longer. They were specifically designed to do that! These days, you'll be lucky to get 10 years. And that's with excellent maintenance and timely repairs.

Anticipate So You Are Not Caught off Guard

Anticipate costs to repair and eventually replace major home appliances. Create a special account designated just for future appliance replacement. Setting aside a small amount of money every month will give you cash options to make wise decisions when the time comes.

7 Ways to Use Borax

A recent letter from a reader who used borax to solve her dishwasher woes got me thinking about all the ways I use this handy product to clean and fix problems around the house.

What Is Borax?

Borax is actually a salt that is found naturally in evaporation lakes. It is used as an ingredient in many detergents, cosmetics and enamel glazes. You can find it in supermarkets, in the laundry or cleaning aisles, and online under many different brand names.

Precautions To Take

Be careful about dumping large amounts into a container and breathing in the dust. You should never do this with anything that is a fine powder, not just borax.

Keep borax in a sealed container away from children, just as you do with ANY cleaning agent, even natural ones.

Do not use borax for skin care or topical use. It is really for cleaning only. And remember this: More is not better. You only need a small amount of borax to get any number of jobs done.

No. 1: Clean Carpet

Borax is a natural odor neutralizer, which makes it a perfect option for cleaning carpets by hand or boosting the cleaning power of your carpet machine. It will make those carpets smell even better.

No. 2: Garbage Disposal

Once a week or so, and between deep garbage disposal cleanings, sprinkle 4 tablespoons of borax into the disposal. Allow to sit for 30 minutes to soak up grease, bad odors and other nasty things that build up inside that appliance. Next, pour a pot of boiling water into the disposal while it runs for a few seconds to dislodge everything. This will keep the disposal clean and prevent it from getting stinky.

No. 3: Unclog a Drain

Got a slow-running drain? Unclog it with 1/2 cup of borax in the drain followed by 2 cups of boiling water. Let that sit for 30 minutes or so, and then follow with warm water to flush that clog away.

No. 4: Scouring Cleanser

Use borax straight-up for a very effective scouring powder to scrub your sinks, tubs and stovetops.

No. 5: Car Upholstery

Mix up a batch of this homemade upholstery cleaner:

3 tablespoons Dawn dishwashing liquid

3 tablespoon borax

3 cups boiling water

Mix all ingredients in a small saucepan over high heat, and bring it to a boil. Remove from stove and allow to cool slightly, but only until you can touch it. You want to use this when it's as hot as is tolerable. With a good scrubber like a sponge or brush, scrub your car's upholstery. Use it on the floor mats, too! Rinse with cool water and a clean rag.

Pro tip: This is a great cleaner for any upholstery, not only in a vehicle.

No. 6: Bathroom Cleaner

There are tons of DIY bathroom cleaner recipes out there, but none can top this one, in my humble opinion!

1/2 cup white vinegar

2 tablespoons borax

1 tablespoon blue Dawn dishwashing liquid

2 cups warm water

10 drops lemon essential oil (optional, but adds a lovely clean scent)

Pour all ingredients into a spray bottle, and shake to mix.

This works really well on ceramic tile, the outside surfaces of toilets, sinks, counters and floors.

Note: Do not use this cleaner on natural stone. Vinegar is an acid and can eat away at stone and marble surfaces overtime. Stone tiles, travertine, granite, marble or anything in that family should not have vinegar as a cleaner.

No. 7: All-Purpose Cleaner

Pour these ingredients into a spray bottle:

1 teaspoon borax

1/2 teaspoon washing soda

1 teaspoon Blue Dawn or castile soap

18 drops lemon essential oil

Fill the bottle to the top with hot water, and shake until everything is mixed well. This cleaner is perfect for greasy messes, fingerprints and smudges.

How to Redecorate on a Dime

Changing your environment can greatly improve your outlook. And that doesn't have to cost a fortune. The key to great decor isn't how much money you spend. It's about seeing the possibilities in what you have already. You'll be surprised at what you can do for little or no cost.

Use What You've Got

I have a friend who calls herself a professional arranger because people hire her to come to their homes and "redecorate" with the things they already have. She goes through every room, the attic and the basement, taking inventory of everything available for her designs. Then she completely clears the room and starts from scratch to furnish and decorate with only the things she found in the home. The results are amazing.

If that triggered something in you that whispered, "I wish someone would pay me to do that," check out the International Association of Home Staging Professionals. Or offer to do this for a few friends. Take before and after photos, and order business cards. You do not need a license or any particular certification to become a professional arranger.

Paint Is Cheap

Changing the color of one wall can change the entire mood of a room. One quart of paint is all you need. You can fool the eye with the way you use paint, making a room appear larger or smaller simply by changing of color.

It doesn't have to be an entire wall. Paint the inside of drawers, cupboards or closets a bright color to give yourself a fresh reason to keep that space organized. Cool colors and lighter tints make walls look farther apart; rich, dark colors bring walls dramatically closer, creating an intimate look in a large room.

Consider These Tips To Make the Job Easier

Check your local hazardous waste recycling center or the "Goof!" shelves in the paint department at Home Depot for free or low-cost paint. One reader painted her entire house for $45 using three low-cost, five-gallon buckets of brand-new but leftover

high-quality construction paint.

Use an old vinyl tablecloth as a drop cloth, or spend a buck for one at a dollar store. They are heavier than the plastic drop cloths at home centers like Lowe's and Home Depot and will last for many rooms of painting. When you're done, just hose it off and hang it over a clothesline or fence to dry before folding and storing.

When you take off the outlet and switch the covers, put the screws back into the holes so they don't get lost. Or put the covers and screws in a sandwich bag.

Line your roller pan with a plastic grocery bag (inside out if it has printing on it) on the paint tray. Then you can just invert the bag when you're done and throw it away.

Clean your brushes with a dryer sheet. A glass jar works great for this. Stuff the dryer sheet into it, and then fill with warm water. Place the brushes' bristles down into the water, and allow to stand for three to four hours. Rinse brushes well, and dry.

Strategic Placement

The furniture you use most should be farthest from the entrance. If possible, avoid positioning couches, chairs, dining tables or desks against walls. Give yourself at least 3 feet between the furniture and walls. Check out these no-fail tricks for arranging furniture.

Pictures and Art

Most people hang pictures and art too high. The focal point for a single picture or the center of a group of pictures should be at eye-level for a person who is 5 feet, 7 inches tall. If that's not you, I'll bet you know someone who is that height.

Plants

Houseplants should be right for the light available in the area where you want to display them. Some easy growers that don't require a lot of extra care include Philodendron and Boston fern.

Microfiber Cloths and Why They Work Like Magic

There's nothing like microfiber for cleaning just about any surface in and around the house. If you've never used a microfiber cloth, you're going to be amazed by how fast and efficiently you can clean.

Housecleaning and Car Washing

They're chores that most of us love to hate. Who would have thought there could ever be a better way to scrub things clean than using good old soap and water plus an old, ratty cotton cloth?

If you've tried the latest microfiber cleaning cloths, you know that technology really can make life easier. Microfiber cloths are not only more hygienic but also less expensive. You'll avoid the need for expensive cleaning products, which are often laden with strong chemicals that, for some, cause allergic reactions and skin problems.

Microfiber cloths get things looking far cleaner in a lot less time—especially windows, mirrors, stainless steel and dishes. It's not magic. It's science.

Adhesive Forces

Microfibers, made of polyester and polyamide, are able to attach themselves to even the smallest, most microscopic dirt particles—ones that normal cloth fibers (gigantic by comparison) rudely brush past. If these forces were visible, you'd be able to see that there are "adhesive" forces that create a strong attraction between those teeny-tiny fibers and dirt.

Dusting Magnet

For household dusting, use a microfiber cloth dry, as you would a traditional dusting rag. But look how differently it works. A regular rag moves dust from one spot to another. But a microfiber cloth? It acts like a magnet. You have to see this.

Damp Cleaning

But for more general cleaning, you always want microfiber to be damp, even when using it to dry a surface. The first time you use a microfiber cloth, force of habit will have you soaking it with water, adding soap and then wringing it out, which only reduces the cloth's effectiveness.

The best way to use these cloths for normal cleaning is with as little water as possible. You can use microfiber cloths to clean virtually any hard surface. Try them on your bathroom or kitchen surfaces, and you'll be amazed at the results.

Dirty Situations

If you're dealing with a fairly dirty situation, follow this two-step practice: Use a regular cloth and soapy water or your favorite all-purpose cleaner to wash all the dirt off first. Rinse. Now polish over it with your damp microfiber cloth.

Notice the smear-free, sparkling finish. Sorry to sound like a bad TV commercial, but these things are really good! I think you'll agree once you see things getting squeaky clean and shiny with so little effort.

70/30 Is Best

Microfiber cloths come in varying sizes and grades to clean every surface imaginable, from eyeglasses and countertops to windows and cars. The best microfiber cloths are made of at least 70% polyester and 30% polyamide. There are plenty of fakes and poor-quality microfiber cloths out there, so it's good to know what to look for to know you're not wasting your money on junk.

If you wash and dry microfiber properly (never use fabric softeners with microfiber) and keep them in good condition, you'll have them for many years to come. Microfiber just doesn't wear out like traditional fabric.

How To Launder

Because microfiber picks up dust and dirt germs so effectively, it is mandatory that you remove everything that gets stuck in those tiny, magnetlike fibers—much of which is not visible to the naked eye. You have to thoroughly clean microfiber cloths after you've used them. Follow the manufacturer's washing instructions.

Surprisingly, the best way is to boil a microfiber cloth in a saucepan on the stovetop to avoid washing with regular detergents. This way, "washing" with water only, you will kill bacteria, germs and viruses without leaving any residues behind. Hang to dry.

Pro Tip

Never, ever use any kind of laundry softener on microfiber. If you use detergent or soap of any kind, make triple sure it is thoroughly rinsed out so that absolutely no residue remains.

7 Houseplants That Are Really Hard to Kill

I love houseplants, and I do have some beauties! The truth is I don't have a green thumb; I just know a few tricks and tips that I will gladly share with you. Healthy, beautiful houseplants are an economical way to bring instant warmth and beauty to a home, condo, apartment, dorm room, recreational vehicle—or wherever else you call home.

I have friends who, I swear, were born with a green thumb. These talented people effortlessly grow lush, beautiful, exotic plants indoors. Then, there are the rest of us.

Here's my best-kept horticultural secret: I only consider plants in what I call the "thrivus neglectus" family, which comes from the Latin root meaning "really cheap and thrives even under the harshest conditions of poor light and owner neglect."

Know Your Varieties

If growing beautiful houseplants in your home or office isn't your forte, I have good news. It is possible to have lovely plants if you pick the right variety—those that are hard to kill.

Peace lily: The indoor plant spathiphyllum, with its graceful nickname "peace lily," is an easy-care, low-light houseplant. It's beautiful, lush and fast-growing. Can you see a peace lily in every room?

Cast-iron plant: Aspidistra is also known as the "cast-iron plant," and for good reason. This baby can survive any condition, including low light and a dry environment. It has earned its nickname because it can survive in deep shade and does not like direct sun or extreme cold.

Devil's ivy: Epipremnum aureum, commonly called "pothos" or "devil's ivy," comes in many varieties that tolerate poor light and actually enjoy being left alone. Nearly fuss-free, this lush, leafy evergreen pothos plant will tolerate a range of indoor growing conditions, including heat, aridity and dry shade.

Rubber plant: Ficus elastica, or "rubber plant," likes a cool, dimly lit space. But if you should happen to set it in a sunny area, watch out. It will grow like crazy, and you'll be searching on the internet for how to prune the darned thing!

Spider plant: Also known as chlorophytum comosum, "spider plant" is tough and does well in low light. It sends out these really cool trailing vines that develop tiny dangling baby "spiders" instead of flowers. Really cool!

Corn plant: Dracaena, or "corn plant," is a great choice for hot, dry apartments. This plant is a popular ornamental houseplant, grown both indoors and outdoors in subtropical climates. Bright indirect light is best for corn plant. Too much light can cause the leaves to burn. It reaches a height of about 3 feet indoors and has a bushy tree type of look. A corn plant's glossy leaves can grow up to 1 foot long and a couple of inches wide.

Mother-in-law's tongue: The ever-popular sansevieria trifasciata, nicknamed "snake plant" or "mother-in-law's tongue" (best nickname ever), likes full sun to low light source and even moisture. It will survive even under the most severely neglectful conditions. Sansevieria trifasciata is prized for its stiff, upright leaves that range from 1 to 8 feet tall, depending on the variety.

Know Where To Buy

I'm a huge fan of the Walmart and Target garden departments. Home improvement centers like Home Depot and Lowe's are excellent sources as well. Just look for the bargain table and you'll run right into the plants on my list above.

Know When To Water

Unlike silk and plastic, live houseplants do require water, and watering weekly is good. Pick a day, any day—and then water your plants on the same day every week. Don't overdo it.

Know Your Maintenance

Keep the leaves of your plants clean. Dust plugs the pores and prevents plants from taking in the carbon dioxide from the air. A damp cloth once every few weeks will do the trick.

Live plants are an inexpensive way to create a warm and welcoming atmosphere in any living space. As a bonus, they improve indoor air quality.

Select plants that require little or no care, and you'll save yourself both time and money.

A Simple Solution for Gross, Smelly Towels

If my inbox is any indicator of what's going on in the world, and I believe it is, smelly towels are a growing problem for consumers—and certainly for my dear "Everyday Cheapskate" readers. And it's a rather new problem, the result of modern things like front-loading high-efficiency washing machines, detergents, fabric softeners and damp conditions.

If you've noticed gross, smelly towels in your houses, albeit appearing to be washed, dried and ready to go, perhaps you've also noticed that your towels have begun to repel rather than absorb water.

Smell

That moldy, mildewy, gross smell? It's the result of the buildup of detergents and fabric softeners that have not been rinsed out properly, together with damp, moist conditions. What you have there is a breeding ground for bacteria. No wonder you've got a big, gross, smelly laundry problem.

Absorbency

If your towels have stopped doing what they're supposed to do well—absorb water—that problem stems from the same source: detergent and fabric softener buildup. Seriously! With detergent and laundry, more is decidedly not better.

Science

You are going to use white vinegar and baking soda to fix this skanky problem once and for all. But do not use these products at the same time. This will be a two-step process.

Vinegar contains acetic acid that breaks down mineral deposits and dissolves the buildup of detergent and fabric softeners. Baking soda is alkaline and breaks down dirt and grease and neutralizes odors. Used together, they counteract each other.

For this process, we want them to do their work independently. This will strip the residue and leave them fresh and able to absorb more water again.

Wash No. 1

Load towels into the washer loosely. Set it for a long wash

cycle and fill with the hottest water you can manage. Turn the water heater up to 140 F for this event, or boil water on the stovetop and carefully transport it to the washer. The point is that the water must be very hot to kill the bacteria. Add 2 cups of white vinegar to the load. Allow it to run the entire cycle and then leave the towels in the washer.

Wash No. 2

Fill the machine once more with the hottest water possible. This time, add 1 cup of baking soda. Run the entire cycle.

Dry Completely

Whether you hang the towels outdoors or put them in the dryer, make sure they are completely and thoroughly dry. Now smell them. If they do not smell fabulously clean, repeat Wash No. 1 and Wash No. 2 as necessary, until the odor is completely gone. The investment you've made in these towels makes them worth the effort.

Maintenance

Find your owners manual, and discover the exact amount of detergent you should be using in your washing machine. Measure it every time. Never add more than recommended, especially if you have a front-loading, high-efficiency machine that uses very little water.

Never use softening products—liquid softener or dryer sheets—on your towels. These products coat the fibers with a thin layer of chemicals, which make towels less absorbent and prone to produce buildup, aka smelly towels!

Instead, add 1/2 cup of white vinegar to the last rinse. This will get out the last of the detergent, which causes towels to become scratchy, and prevent that horrid product buildup that can turn smelly.

How to Get Yellow-Stained Bed Pillows White Again

Favorite bed pillows get a lot of use every night. We keep clean pillowcases on them and don't think much about the pillow inside until it's time to change the bed linens. Have you looked lately?

What Are Those Stains?

The culprit is sweat, the chemical composition of which varies from one person to the next depending on everything from what that person has been eating to what medications he or she is taking. Now add drool, body oils, makeup and hair products transferred to the pillow from lying down with wet hair; all of these things discolor pillows over time. But why not the pillowcase? Because we launder them frequently, so stains are banished quickly before they have a chance to become a problem.

If your pillow has a zippered pillow liner, remove it. You're in luck if the stains are limited to just that protective cover (this is different from a pillowcase and often comes with the pillow). If the pillow itself has stains, it's time to wash both the liner and the pillow.

Washable Pillows Only

Check to make sure the pillow tag says that it is washable. Most pillows can be safely washed. (Do not attempt to wash memory-foam pillows.) Wash only one large (king-size) pillow or two smaller pillows at a time for the best results.

You'll need these ingredients:

Soilove (or your favorite laundry pretreatment stain remover)

1 cup powdered laundry detergent

1 cup powdered automatic dishwasher detergent

1/2 cup borax

1 cup bleach (or bleach alternative)

1 cup white vinegar

Step 1

Treat the stains and allow them to sit for about 20 minutes.

Step 2

Soak the pillows in a large container filled with hot water—the hottest you can manage from the tap. If your washing machine is a top-loader and has a soak function, use that. Fill the washer with hot water and then stop the cycle to allow the pillow(s) to soak. For front-loading machines, you'll need to use a big basin or the bathtub.

Step 3

While the pillows soak, pull out the biggest cooking pot you can find. Fill it with tap water, set it on a burner on high, and bring it to full boil. Turn the burner off, and pour in the laundry detergent, dishwasher detergent and borax. Stir gently until the products dissolve in the boiling water.

Step 4

Carefully pour the contents of your hot caldron into the washer, storage bin or tub—wherever your pillows are soaking. Carefully add and stir in the liquid bleach. Make sure the stained pillows are fully saturated by turning them over or moving them around. You may need to use a broom handle or similar to gently push them down in the washer, as pillows will tend to float. Allow soaking for at least one hour. Longer is fine.

Step 5

After the soak, launder the pillow(s) using your machine's longest hot wash cycle, with an extra rinse if you have that option. Add a cup of white vinegar to the final rinse by pouring it into the liquid softener reservoir. This will keep it separate from the bleach, as you do not want to mix bleach and vinegar.

Step 6

Dry the pillows in the dryer in a medium heat cycle along with wool dryer balls if you have them. If not, throw a couple of tennis balls, each one tied into the toe of a sock, into the dryer to keep the pillows moving. For down pillows, use the air-only or fluff option. If the pillow is synthetic, use low heat.

Keep Them White

Get some zippered pillow protectors. A great idea is to use two of these on each pillow—one to protect the pillow and one to act as a pillowcase. Now, as you change and launder your bed linens, peel off the pillowcase and do an inspection. If you see any spots on the top pillow protector, launder it, too. Inspect the second protector. If it's white and pristine, you're good to go. If not, into the laundry it goes.

Check your pillows routinely so you can deal with spots quickly. That's the secret to keeping pillows white and pristine!

How to Clean Leather Furniture

When it comes to furnishing your home, it's difficult to find anything more luxurious and elegant than fine leather. With that elegance comes the challenge of how to clean it and maintain it so it gets even better with age.

If your leather furniture is stained or looking a little on the tired side, follow these suggestions to perk it up.

Type of Leather

First, determine the type of leather you're working with. You want to know if it is aniline or top-coated. Typically, this information will be found on the tags or the brochure you were given when you acquired the item.

Aniline Leather

This type of leather is dyed exclusively with soluble dyes. The dye colors the leather without producing a topcoat or sealant. Aniline leather is a natural leather that has a very soft finish, is very absorbent and stains easily. Do everything you can to keep it free of stains and spills.

Top-Coated Leather

This is the most commonly used finishing technique for leather used to upholster furniture and automobile seats. The finish consists of an opaque base coat followed by a protective topcoat. Since the natural color of the leather is covered completely, the leather can be identified by its uniform color.

Most leather furniture these days has top-coat protected leather, which is usually safe to clean as follows:

Vacuum

Remove all the loose dirt, dust and debris from the item to be cleaned. A vacuum with the soft brush attachment is the best option, as it will get into the seams and crevices. Be gentle, though. Leather is delicate, and you don't want to scratch it as you are vacuuming.

Treat Stains

Before you do a general cleaning, you want to treat, and hopefully remove, any stains.

For food, blood or other dark stains—even those whose origin you're not sure of—make a paste of 1 part cream of tartar and 1 part lemon juice. Rub this paste on the stain, and allow it to sit for 10 minutes. Remove the paste with a damp rag and moisturizing soap (as described below). Rinse. Dry. And buff the leather dry with a soft cloth.

Clean

Mix a few drops of a mild liquid facial cleanser or body wash, such as Dove Body Wash, Neutrogena Facial Cleanser or any shampoo that does not contain sodium laurel sulfate (a harsh ingredient that could dry out the leather), with 1 quart of distilled water until suds form (chlorine and other contaminants in regular tap water can damage the surface).

Test

Using a soft white cloth, test this cleaner in an inconspicuous place by scrubbing a small area. Observe how the leather responds.

Dive In

Assuming the test gives a good result, dip the soft, clean white cloth into the soapy water, and wring it out thoroughly. Working on a small section at a time, apply it to the surface of the furniture with the damp rag.

Rinse

Dip another soft, clean white rag into clean distilled water. Wring it out thoroughly. Then wipe away the soap residue.

Dry

Immediately dry the area using yet another soft, clean white rag.

Buff

With a fourth soft, clean white cloth, buff well to restore the luster.

Condition

Treat the surface with a nontoxic high-quality leather protector/conditioner, such as the Leather Rescue Conditioner, carefully following the label instructions. Trust me, this stuff is awesome. Not only does it rescue and restore the appearance of leather; it covers scratches, too!

Maintain

Never use harsh cleaners or any kind of oil, furniture polish, baby wipes, household cleaners or products containing wax or silicone on your leather furniture. These could damage and/or leave the surface feeling sticky.

Position Properly

To keep your fine leather furniture from fading, drying out or cracking, avoid placing it in direct sunlight. Keep it at least 2 feet from anything that produces heat like heating vents, fireplaces, radiators and air conditioning sources.

Always Test First

Be sure to always test any treatment in an inconspicuous area, especially with aniline leather.

How to Clean and Care for Hardwood and Laminate Floors

Taking care of hardwood or laminate floors can be challenging given the everyday conditions of a family and pets.

Generally, there are two types of residential wood flooring: real wood (solid or engineered) and laminate that is man-made to look like wood.

Don't know what you have exactly? No worries. When it comes to cleaning wood floors (solid, engineered or laminate), the only thing you need to figure out is whether or not your floors have a finish. You don't really need to know the type of finish, just whether the floors have been treated to make them resistant to standing water, which is the enemy of all wood and woodlike floors.

Drop-Of-Water Test

To find out if your flooring is finished, drop a single drop of water on the floor. If it beads and just sits there, the flooring has been finished. If the drop soaks in and disappears, leaving a dark spot, the wood is not finished.

What follows is for finished solid or engineered wood and laminate flooring only. Unfinished hardwood CANNOT be mopped, since the floors will be damaged.

If your floor is unfinished, or if it's an old wood floor and some of the finish has started to wear away, then don't use any moisture or product. Just dust mop it with a flat-head mop.

Wood Floor Cleaners

When it comes to wood and laminate cleaners, you can spend a fortune on commercial products like Bona Black Diamond. Or you can make your own for pennies.

The key to making your own is similar to the commitment of a physician: First, do no harm. The trick is making a product that will clean well without harming the finish, even when used repeatedly over many years.

No Vinegar

White vinegar is a fabulous cleaning product because it cuts through dirt well. But it is highly acidic and, used repeatedly over time, can attack the finish, making your floors look dull. Vinegar can also soften the finish, making it feel gummy or sticky. So, let's just agree that when it comes to cleaning wood or laminate floors, no vinegar.

Yes, Alcohol

Alcohol is also a fantastic cleaning product—rubbing alcohol (70% is most common, but 91% works is great, too), denatured alcohol, even gin or plain vodka. It has a nearly neutral pH—neither acidic nor alkaline. This makes alcohol the perfect ingredient in your homemade cleaner to not only clean but also protect and preserve beautifully finished wood and laminate floors.

Distilled Water

Use distilled water in your floor cleaner (available in any supermarket) to eliminate streaking, hard watermarks and mineral buildup.

Blue Dawn

A very small amount of Blue Dawn—not so much that it requires rinsing—will break the surface tension of the water, making the cleaner much more effective.

Homemade Wood and Laminate Floor Cleaner

It's 1 part alcohol to 4 parts distilled water plus a few drops blue Dawn dishwashing liquid. Here it is again:

1 part alcohol
4 parts distilled water
2 or 3 drops Blue Dawn

Example: 1/4 cup alcohol, 1 cup distilled water, 2 drops Blue Dawn.

Mix this up in a spray bottle each time you clean the floors. If you make it ahead of time, be sure to label it well and keep it out of the reach of children.

How To Clean

Sweep or vacuum the floor. Spray the cleaner in a small area. Scrub well with a cloth or sponge. And immediately wipe the area dry with a microfiber cloth.

The secret is to spray, scrub and wipe dry immediately. If

you do not want to do this on your hands and knees, I recommend using a microfiber spray mop, which works well on both wood and laminate floors.

Taking good care of your wood and laminate floors will not only keep your home looking great; you'll be protecting your home's value, which is likely one of the biggest investments you will ever make.

Food and Recipes

Cleverly Delicious Ways to Use Up Leftovers

If your refrigerator is at all like mine, it harbors an odd assortment of leftovers and "almost gones." After all, it's hard to throw out what appears to be perfectly good food, but what can you do with a little of this and not very much of that? Here are some suggestions that may get your creative juices flowing to come up with your own ideas for what's lurking in your refrigerator.

Bottled Salad Dressing

It's a rare refrigerator that doesn't have an assortment of almost empty salad dressing bottles. Here's what you can do with any oil and vinegar based dressings like Caesar, Italian or other vinaigrettes, even the low-fat varieties: Mix all of those small amounts together in one bottle, then label for marinade for beef, pork or chicken. The oil adds flavor, and the vinegar (or another acid such as lemon juice) tenderizes. You need enough to coat the meat or poultry, then cover and refrigerate for at least an hour before roasting, grilling or baking.

Applesauce

That last bit of applesauce in the jar will make a wonderful coleslaw dressing. Make sure you have about 1/2 cup applesauce left in the jar and then add about 1/2 cup mayonnaise, 1/4 teaspoon onion powder, 1/3 teaspoon celery salt, 1 teaspoon prepared mustard, 1 teaspoon sugar and 2 tablespoons water. Apply the lid and shake well. To use: Toss with about 4 cups shredded cabbage or packaged coleslaw mix. Refrigerate overnight to allow flavors to meld. Yield: 8 servings.

Mashed Potatoes

Leftover mashed potatoes make a great topper for almost any casserole, such as Shepherd's Pie, for example. Preheat the oven to 400 F. In a skillet, heat 1 tablespoon olive oil and saute 1 pound ground or shredded turkey (you can also use chicken, beef or other meat), 1/4 cup minced celery and 1/2 cup chopped onion until brown. Add 3/4 cup beef or chicken broth, 1 tablespoon ketchup, 1/4 teaspoon dry mustard, and 1 teaspoon Worcestershire sauce. Cook for 5 minutes. Mix in frozen or drained canned green peas. Pour mixture into an 8x8 square baking pan. Spread the leftover mashed potatoes over the top. Sprinkle with a little paprika for color (optional). Bake for 30 minutes. Yield: 6 servings.

Cooked Rice

Turn that leftover rice into a wonderful quiche crust. Mix together 2 cups white or brown leftover cooked rice, 1 beaten egg and 1 teaspoon soy sauce. Spread evenly to cover a well-buttered quiche or pie pan. Bake crust at 350 F for 10 minutes. Remove from oven. Place any kind of fresh or frozen vegetables (broccoli is a good choice) or meat on the crust. Mix together 4 beaten eggs, 1 1/2 cups milk or half-and-half, salt and pepper to taste, and a dash of nutmeg. Pour over vegetables and meat. Top with 1 cup grated cheese (Swiss, cheddar, Monterey Jack or any combination). Bake at 350 F for 45 to 50 minutes or until a knife inserted near center of pie comes out clean. Remove from oven and let sit 10 minutes before serving. You can practically clean out the refrigerator right into your quiche pan. Just remember to add the cheese last to make a beautiful, golden-brown crust on the top.

Buttermilk

Lots of recipes call for a fairly small amount of buttermilk. That's great, but what to do with the rest of a quart or pint? That 1/2 cup of buttermilk languishing in the back of the fridge won't last forever. Here's an awesome suggestion: Before it goes bad, use it to make fabulous overfried fish. Preheat the oven to 400 F. Line a baking pan or cookie sheet with aluminum foil and spray it with cooking spray. In a flat dish or pan, mix together 1/2 cup cornmeal, 1/2 teaspoon paprika, 1/2 teaspoon oregano, 1/8 teaspoon cayenne, salt and pepper to taste, stirring with a fork until blended. Pour the buttermilk into a shallow bowl. Cut fish fillets to equal 4 servings into portion-sized pieces (Catfish is perfect for this recipe, but any white fish works really well.) Dip each piece in the buttermilk and then in the cornmeal mixture, making sure to dip both sides of each piece. Place on the sprayed foil. Drizzle olive oil over the fillets or spray with olive oil-flavored cooking spray. Bake for 25 minutes.

How to Regrow Scallions and Other Vegetables from Scraps

At our house, we're getting much better with storing and using up produce. In fact, we've all but completely stopped throwing rotten produce into the garbage. Now, I'm taking it further by actually regrowing vegetables from scraps—in the kitchen window! It's like my inner gardener has come out to play, and not a moment too soon as grocery prices soar and inflation in the U.S. has now reached a 20-year high.

Let's start with scallions (green onions). They're extremely useful, deliciously versatile and dirt cheap. Invariably, I either fail to use them up completely before they go bad or I run out, prompting quick trips to the market, which exposes my impulsive self to at least a few unplanned purchases. But no more now that I have a tiny crop of fresh scallions growing on my kitchen windowsill. It's so easy to keep the white ends in a glass of water where they sprout and regrow into new, fresh scallions.

Here are some simple steps to regrow scallions:

No. 1: Stand the white parts of the scallions, with the wispy root ends down, in a glass or jar.

No. 2: Add water to cover the roots.

No. 3: Set the container in a sunny window.

No. 4: Change the water every day or two.

In a week or so, you can begin harvesting the green ends of the scallions, depending on how much green you started with. Snip what you need with a pair of kitchen scissors (you can take up to 70% of the green part) and leave the rest to keep growing. The green part of the scallion will regrow itself. You'll save money and frustration, and have yourself a fun, low-maintenance and edible windowsill pet.

While scallions are the easiest vegetable to regrow, this method works with other vegetables.

Lettuce

Don't expect a full head of lettuce from your windowsill garden, but you can get a few leaves at a time, which is enough for a sandwich or garnish.

Put the stem end of the head, with a few inches of the lettuce intact, in a shallow dish of water. Place it in a window area that gets plenty of sunlight. Keep the water fresh by changing it every one to two days.

Celery

A few tender, delicious stalks will regrow—just enough for most dishes that call for celery.

Similar to the steps above for regenerating lettuce, place the stem end in a shallow dish of water by a sunny window. Change the water frequently.

You'll get better results with celery when you poke toothpicks into the sides of the celery to prop it up. You want to submerge the celery, but keep the bottom from touching the dish to give the roots plenty of room to breathe.

Fennel

You can grow back the green shoots of a fennel bulb by following the same steps for lettuce and celery. Place the bulb end, with the root system still intact, in shallow water, and wait for the plant to begin to regrow.

Herbs

A wide range of herbs works well to regrow using cuttings and scraps. Start with a stem that is about 4 inches in length in a glass of water, making sure to remove all leaves below the water level.

You will learn how to make full use of a plant's ability to grow new roots and regenerate itself to help you reduce the amount of food waste that you generate in your home.

How to Upsize a Cake Mix That's Too Small for the Recipe

In my kitchen, I have a small collection of cookbooks which I consider prized possessions. One of them, the classic Betty Crocker Cookbook, was a wedding gift and, trust me, it's seen more than its share of splatters and dog-eared and ripped pages. And I wouldn't part with it for anything.

Another features 100 things to do with an ordinary cake mix. It is fabulous—or I should say it used to be.

Here's the problem: About five years ago, cake mix manufacturers got the bright idea to shrink the contents of a standard cake mix rather than increase the price. Sneaky, right? And what a terrible decision that was. What used to be the standard 18.25 ounce cake mix suddenly shrunk to 15.25 ounces. Have you noticed this?

That might not be a problem if you're using that cake mix to make the cake according to the back-of-the-box instructions, which is going to turn out noticeably smaller, by the way. But if you're into hacking a cake mix (where the mix becomes a single ingredient in a much better recipe for anything from waffles, to cookies, to much-improved cake), it's a problem. Those recipes in my little "100 Things" cookbook all assume an 18.25 ounce cake mix. And why not? That's the way it had been for decades.

Does it really matter? It does, because unlike cooking a pot roast or lasagna where exact measurements are not critical, baking relies on chemical reactions. Exact measurements do matter.

But there's good news! If your cake mix is too small, it's easy to remedy. Here are three options:

Method No. 1

Purchase two 15.25 ounce cake mixes. Add 3 ounces (6 tablespoons) from the second mix to make up the difference. Keep the balance of that second mix in a tightly sealed container to use the next time you make this cake.

Method No. 2

Purchase a plain yellow cake mix and empty its contents into a glass mason jar. Keep it tightly covered and stored in the pantry. When you need to supplement any flavor cake mix so that it is a full 18.25 ounces, remove 3 ounces of the yellow cake mix and add to the 15.25 ounce cake mix. Yellow cake mix has a neutral flavor, so this is not going to adversely affect the outcome.

Method No. 3

Make your own "Cake Mix Upsizer." To upsize white and yellow cake mixes:

1 1/2 cups all-purpose flour
1 cup sugar
2 teaspoons baking powder
1/4 teaspoon baking soda

To upsize chocolate mixes:

1 cup and 2 tablespoons all-purpose flour
1 cup sugar
6 tablespoons cocoa powder
2 teaspoons baking powder
1/4 teaspoon baking soda

Whisk all dry ingredients together and store in a clean mason jar. When you wish to increase a 15.25 ounce cake mix to 18.25 ounces, add 3 ounces of this mix to your existing cake mix. Store that remainder in a tightly closed container, like a glass canning jar with a lid, on the pantry shelf. Yield: About 6 portions.

There you go—a fairly simple remedy for a very annoying problem. Happy baking!

How to Liquify Crystallized Honey and the Best Way to Store It

It's discouraging when you reach for the honey, only to discover it is no longer a smooth liquid, but all grainy—like sugar. You may have even tossed it into the trash assuming that it's gone bad, no longer edible. Truth be told, it is still perfectly delicious and nutritious. It's easy to turn crystallized honey back into its liquid self.

First, if your crystallized honey is in a plastic container, transfer as much as you want to liquify to a glass container with a lid. Apply the lid. Then, you have three choices:

No. 1: Stovetop Method

Set a pan of water over high heat and bring it to a boil. Turn off the burner and allow the water to cool for about 5 minutes, or until it is below 140 F. Set the honey in the water. Cover the pan. Check after an hour or so, stirring the honey as needed.

No. 2: Slow Cooker Method

Set the covered honey into the slow cooker. Add enough water to cover the honey container halfway. Cover the slow cooker and set it to low. After 30 minutes or so, check the water temperature to make sure it is not above 140 F. If it is, add a little cold water. If not, allow it to continue until the honey is liquid.

No. 3: Sous Vide Method

If you have a sous vide cooker, place the tightly closed honey container in the water. Set the sous vide to 140 F. Allow it to cook for several hours, as needed to achieve liquid honey.

What Is the Best Way to Store Honey?

Normal room temperature is ideal for honey, where it will not be subject to getting moisture inside. If your house tends to get warm, find the coolest spot in the pantry for it. Keep it away from the stove and other heat-producing appliances, as well as sunlight.

Why Does Honey Crystallize or Become "Sugared"?

The answer is temperature. When the temperature where the honey is stored drops below 50 F (10 C), crystals appear. That process starts at 57 F but becomes visible below 50 F. The longer it remains below 50 F, the more crystals will form until it is mostly solid. Cloudy or crystallized honey is nothing to worry about.

Is Crystallized Honey Edible?

Absolutely, yes! In fact, some people prefer their honey in a more solid, spreadable state. The flavor is the same whether liquid or crystallized.

Can I Decrystallize Honey in the Microwave?

No. That's because it is too difficult to monitor and measure the temperature of the decrystallizing process using a microwave oven. It is not a reliable method because it gets too hot, too quickly. Your results will be, at best, sketchy. At most? You will have destroyed the honey's benefits and changed its flavor. Been there; done that; will not repeat.

Honey Is Life-Sustaining

Honey is the only food source that contains everything to sustain human life. It contains antioxidants, vitamins and minerals that we need, even water.

Honey is Medicinal

Honey is good to treat diaper rashes, stomach ulcers, burns and seasonal allergies (although the honey you are taking must be from the same area that you live to be useful in the latter way). Honey has long been known to help relieve sore throats when mixed with lemon juice.

Honey Never Spoils

You never have to throw honey out—even if it has become crystallized. Honey was found in King Tut's tomb that was still good to eat.

Honey Is Effective Against Acne

Organic honey can be effective against acne—and a lot cheaper than those high-priced drugstore cleansers and creams. Spoon some honey into your hands, hold a few seconds to get it nice and warm and coat the problem area. Wait at least five minutes, and then rinse with a soft, warm washcloth. In no time, you are likely to see the difference.

Honey Is Good for Your Skin

Plagued by dry skin, fine lines and wrinkles? Apply honey,

leave it on for 30 minutes and gently wash it away with warm water. Honey may soon become your best friend!

Honey Is Soothing

If you suffer from anxiety, nervousness or the inability to get a good night's sleep, try honey. Add 1 to 2 tablespoons of honey to a mug of hot water. Stir and enjoy!

My Great Pizza Challenge

There are some who consider pizza the perfect food. It has complex carbohydrates, vegetables, dairy and protein. OK, maybe "perfect" is stretching it a bit, but I remember when pizza was something you shouldn't eat too much of because it might spoil your dinner. Now it is dinner.

Millions of families rely on pizza because it is quick and convenient. But is it? To find out, I conducted a less-than-scientific test earlier this week.

I ordered a large 14-inch thin-crust tomato and cheese pizza from Domino's for delivery. As soon as I hung up the phone, I went to work on my homemade pizza with a no-rise crust.

Homemade Pizza

4 teaspoons olive oil
2 teaspoons cornmeal
1 package dry yeast
1 teaspoon sugar
1/2 cup plus 2 tablespoons warm water
2 1/2 cups unbleached all-purpose flour
Salt
1 clove garlic, finely minced
3/4 pound Roma tomatoes, sliced thinly
2 ounces Parmesan cheese, grated
2 tablespoons fresh basil, chopped

Preheat oven to 425 F. Rub 1 teaspoon olive oil over a 14-inch pizza pan, and sprinkle with cornmeal. Stir yeast and sugar into warm water, and let stand until foamy (2-3 minutes).

Combine flour, salt and 1 teaspoon olive oil in food processor bowl fitted with metal blade (this dough can be made with an electric mixer or in a bread machine, although a food processor is ideal). Turn on machine. Pour yeast mixture through feed tube. Process until dough cleans inside of work bowl. If dough sticks, add more flour, a tablespoon at a time. If dough is crumbly, add water a teaspoon at a time. When you reach desired consistency, process dough until uniformly supple and elastic, about 40 seconds.

Roll dough immediately on heavily floured board into a 14-inch circle. If dough resists, let rest 5 minutes to relax gluten, and then try again.

Transfer dough to pizza pan. Work the edge to form rim. Brush with remaining oil. Sprinkle on minced garlic, and cover with an even layer of tomato slices. Sprinkle with Parmesan cheese. Bake for 15-18 minutes until crust is crisp and golden-brown. Sprinkle with fresh basil.

My homemade gourmet-style pizza was out of the oven, sliced and partially consumed before the doorbell rang. It's difficult to give an unbiased opinion on the homemade versus the commercial product because, well, I am anything but impartial. Just let me say that there's nothing like the taste of fresh tomatoes, fresh basil and freshly grated Parmesan cheese on this freshly baked no-rise homemade dough.

Note: You could use a bottled sauce, your favorite toppings and mozzarella cheese to customize to your taste and available ingredients.

As for the time factor, I beat Domino's by a full 20 minutes. And the cost? Mine: less than $4. Domino's: $26, including tip. Homemade for the win!

How to Freeze Eggs, Dairy Products and More

I'm sure my supermarket is not the only grocery store with an area in the back I call "My Bargain Bin." It's refrigerated and features some dandy bargains, especially on perishable items approaching that "sell by" date. There are no limits on the number of items I can load into my cart—all of them with ridiculously low, rock-bottom prices.

You may be asking, "But, Mary, what can we do with all of these perishables to make sure they don't, well, perish?" The answer, of course, is to freeze them. Yes, even the eggs, milk and cheese.

Butter

Freeze margarine or butter in the packaging and containers they come in for up to six months. Thaw to return to their original texture and quality.

Cream, Whipped

Once whipped and sweetened, cream freezes well for one to two months. Note: Freezing cream in its liquid state is not recommended because it affects the quality of the product. In most cases, freezing causes changes to the fat, which can lead to poor texture.

Eggnog

Unopened eggnog may be frozen for up to two months. Thaw in the refrigerator, and shake well before serving, as there may be some ingredient separation during freezing.

Eggs

You can freeze eggs, provided you remove them from the shell first. Do not freeze whole eggs in the shell. Raw eggs can be frozen for up to one year. Thaw in the refrigerator. Hint: Separate the whites from the yolks, and freeze in small portions for easy use.

Milk

Milk may be frozen for as long as three months, provided the saled container is frozen prior to the "best before" date. Skim and low-fat milk freeze better than whole milk. Thaw frozen milk in the refrigerator. The milk will still have the same nutrients, but it may separate. If it does, shake well, and consume as soon as possible.

Cheese

Hard cheese freezes well, but it changes the texture, making it nearly impossible to slice. Frozen cheese is great for cooking and to grate. Hint: Grate first, and then freeze.

Fresh Meat

Fresh beef roasts and steaks can be frozen for up to one year if wrapped well to retard freezer burn; pork and lamb up to six months.

Processed Meats

You can freeze bacon, hot dogs, cooked ham, luncheon meats and sausage for up to two months before these items begin to lose quality and taste.

Fresh Poultry

Whole turkey, chicken, duck and goose can be frozen for up to one year. Poultry pieces, however, should be used within nine months.

Flour

All-purpose flour, whole-wheat flour, cornmeal and other baking staples, including baking powder and baking soda, stay fresh and bug-free indefinitely in the freezer. You will experience no change of texture or taste. Even better? You can ignore the expiration dates.

Coffee and Tea

Storing coffee beans in the freezer has long been the method of choice to preserve freshness. But die-hard coffee lovers tell us to never freeze coffee beans or grinds because it changes the flavor from fresh to "freezer-stale." However, no one argues that freezing leftover brewed coffee in ice cube trays to make blended coffee drinks or iced coffee is a great idea. Freeze leftover tea in the same manner and you'll have "ice" for your iced tea that will not dilute the drink.

Superfoods, Super Cheap

Imagine ordinary food items, available in any supermarket, that are powerful enough to help you lower your cholesterol, reduce your risk of heart disease and cancer, and even put you in a better mood. You'd surely stock up on a lifetime supply and see to it that you add at least one super ingredient to every meal.

Well, imagine no more. Foods that are high in antioxidants, phytoflavinoids and vitamins are available right now in your local supermarket. When you shop smart, superfoods are no more costly than anything else in your grocery cart these days.

A healthy diet incorporating a variety of these superfoods will help you maintain your weight, fight disease and live longer. Here are the top 15 superfoods, all of them real and unprocessed: beans, blueberries, broccoli, brown rice, oats, oranges, pumpkin, tuna, soy, spinach, tea, tomatoes, turkey, walnuts, wild salmon, whole wheat and yogurt.

Here's the secret to eating healthily without breaking the bank: When you see superfoods on sale, load up the freezer and pantry with enough to last until the next sale. Even when they're not on sale, most superfoods are far less costly than processed chips, snacks and carbonated beverages. Let's examine just a handful of these foods so you can get an idea of how they can benefit both you and your wallet:

Brown Rice

This superfood is good for side dishes, rice salads, fried rice, casseroles, soups and stew. Brown rice is high in fiber and protein. Price per serving: 10 cents. A 2-pound bag costs about $3.99 (on sale) and contains 20 servings.

Blueberries

Available year-round frozen, blueberries are packed with antioxidants and phytoflavinoids. Blueberries are also high in potassium and vitamin C, making them the top choice of doctors and nutritionists. They not only lower your risk of heart disease and cancer but also are anti-inflammatory. Price per serving: 66 cents. A 2-pound bag of frozen blueberries costs about $5.99 (on sale) and contains six servings of 1/2 cup each.

Multigrain Pasta

Great in hot or cold pasta dishes, you can substitute whole-wheat pasta in most pasta recipes. One serving (2 ounces uncooked) contains 9 grams of protein and 4 grams of fiber. Got picky eaters? Make the switch gradually by substituting a portion of your regular pasta with whole-wheat. They won't even notice. Price per serving: about 28 cents for a 2-ounce (uncooked) serving. A 13- to 16-ounce box or bag of dried pasta costs about $1.79 to $1.99 (on sale) and contains six to eight servings.

Frozen Vegetables

Serve them alone as a side dish or add frozen vegetables to pasta dishes, soups and stews. Price per serving: around 25 cents for a 1-cup serving. Frozen vegetables come in 12- to 24-ounce bags that cost anywhere from $1.75 to $2.25 and contain 6 to 8 cups, depending on the vegetable and the size of the bag. You can buy a bag of frozen organic green beans at Trader Joe's for $2.79. A bag of petite peas will cost about $2.19, and a 16-ounce bag of frozen chopped spinach costs $2.29.

Canned Tuna

Solid white albacore or chunk light in water is great for sandwiches, casseroles, salads or served straight-up with crackers. One serving (3 ounces) provides about 500 milligrams of omega-3 fatty acids. Price per serving: about 62 cents. You can buy a 5-ounce can for about $1.67 to $1.99, or a 12-ounce can for about $3.99.

Can't figure out how to incorporate superfoods as ingredients in your family's daily menu? Websites such as Allrecipes and MyRecipes have thousands of great recipes that include reviews from other cooks. Or go to the SuperCook website and download the app. Then input the ingredient(s) you want to use, and let SuperCook find just the right recipe for you.

Note: Prices quoted were current at my local Kroger's supermarket at the time of writing.

Kitchen Gadgets That Will Pay for Themselves in No Time at All

I'm crazy about gadgets—everything from quirky can openers to smartphones. Hand me a Swiss Army knife and I'm in heaven—the more blades and utensils the better. And when that gadget is a true money-saver? Oh, be still my heart!

Today, I want to tell you about four gadgets that are inexpensive enough to pay for themselves in a short period of time—and then to continue paying off in food savings, which is saying a lot as food costs continue to soar.

Vacuum Sealer

I've depended on a vacuum sealer in my kitchen for so many years that I cannot imagine getting along without it. Now and then, I get lazy, and invariably, that gives me a jolt to remind me why I do this.

Take strawberries, for example. If I put them into a rigid container (such as a Mason jar using the jar sealer accessory) and vacuum out all of the air, fresh strawberries will last for at least two weeks in the refrigerator—remaining as fresh as the day I bought them. Placed in the refrigerator in their original container, strawberries often start to show mold in just a couple of days.

I vacuum seal raw rice, sugar, spices, meat, baked goods (I freeze them first so the vacuum doesn't crush them), fresh fruits and vegetables.

I vacuum seal silver flatware to keep it from tarnishing. I vacuum sealed my birth certificate and my Social Security card.

A vacuum sealer, when used diligently, will extend the shelf life of every type of food imaginable. That means your garbage disposal and trash can will cease to be the best-fed members of your household!

Blender

I am more convinced than ever that healthy eating is one of the most effective ways to reduce health care costs. That's why I thought we needed a powerful juicer to make healthy smoothies every morning. So, I purchased a highly rated juicer—and used it exactly two times before it became a dust-collector and space-occupier.

Cleaning the thing was so difficult and time-consuming that it became more of a problem than a solution. Whoops.

Another problem? Juicers don't make smoothies! Powerful, professional-grade blenders do.

So, eight years ago, I donated the juicer to a friend who could use it and replaced it with a Blendtec. That exact model Blendtec is still available at a much-reduced price from what I paid.

Dehydrator

No one was more surprised than I by what a terrific money-saver a dehydrator can be. Of course, you have to actually use it. But when you do, you'll be quite amazed.

The cost of dehydrating your own food is a fraction of the cost of commercially dehydrated foods, and it doesn't require any additives or preservatives.

With a good dehydrator around, for about $80, you can dry fruit, vegetables and jerky in hours instead of days.

Food Slicer

I've been using my new electric food slicer for about a year now, and oh, boy, what a lovely item it is. I've pretty much used it every day since I pulled it out of the box. I know what you're thinking: Why?!

I would have asked the same thing before I did a little cost evaluation. At our home, we eat a lot of deli-style turkey—$6.59 per pound at my local Costco. The same brand roast turkey breast unsliced is $3.99 per pound. The exact same thing!

I discovered the same price difference for cheese—sliced versus bulk. After calculating how often I purchase these items, it didn't take long to see that slicing at home would pay off big in lower costs. What I didn't calculate was the fun factor. Seriously, it's fun.

To learn exact brands and models of these kitchen gadgets, go to https://EverydayCheapskate.com/kitchengadgets.

How to Roast a Cheap Cut of Beef

No matter how inexpensive a chuck or round roast may be, if it turns out so tough and flavorless it's passed to the dog, that purchase was no bargain.

And now, thanks to very extensive research and experimentation by Christopher Kimball as reported in Cooks Illustrated magazine, we can confidently purchase those cheaper cuts and expect perfect results every time.

These days, with beef prices hitting all-time highs, buying the cheaper cuts of beef is one way to make our food dollars stretch as far as possible. Just know that what follows is for those of us with more time than money.

When looking for inexpensive cuts, keep these three words in mind: chuck, sirloin and round. The chuck is fattier and more tender; the round is lean and relatively tough. The sirloin falls somewhere between the two.

It was a kick to read the endless details of Kimball's testing. To be quite honest, he lost me somewhere between the five chuck roasts, seven sirloins, eight rounds and endless descriptions of cooking methods, internal temperatures, standing times and lengths of aging.

Curious as I am, I don't care about meat fibers, enzymes or moisture content. And that's when I raced to the conclusion and learned exactly how to prepare a cheap cut of beef. And here it is:

To achieve the best results, you'll need: a rimmed baking sheet with wire rack, a meat thermometer, an oven thermometer and cooking twine or string.

Ingredients

1 boneless beef chuck, sirloin or round roast (3 to 4 1/2 pounds)

4 teaspoons kosher salt, or 2 teaspoons table salt

2 teaspoons plus 2 tablespoons vegetable oil (divided)

2 teaspoons ground black pepper

Exact temperatures are the secret to the best results. For Kimball, varying the oven temperature, internal temperature and cooking times, even slightly, produced roasts that were all the way from slightly dry to so tough they could not be eaten!

The Steps

The following steps are for chuck, sirloin and round cuts of varying size, although 2- to 5-pound roasts are ideal and will produce the best results.

Tie the roast with white cotton string at 1 1/2-inch intervals. Tying the roast tightly makes it compact and shaped evenly, and that's the secret to even roasting.

Pat roast dry with paper towels; rub with 2 teaspoons oil, and sprinkle all sides evenly with salt and pepper. Heat remaining tablespoon oil in a large skillet over medium-high heat until starting to smoke. Sear roast until browned on all sides, 3 to 4 minutes per side. Transfer roast to roasting pan. Place the meat thermometer in the roast so the tip reaches the center of the thickest part. Set the oven thermometer inside the oven close to the pan. Roast uncovered at exactly 250 F until the internal temperature of the roast reaches exactly 130 F (approximately 2 to 2 1/4 hours for a 3- to 4 1/2-pound roast). Remove the pan from the oven, and allow the meat to rest for exactly 20 minutes. Transfer roast to a carving board.

At that moment, according to Kimball, the roast will be succulent, tender, juicy and at its most flavorful. My family and I agree!

How to Make Fruits and Vegetables Last Longer

According to the World Resources Institute, the average U.S. household of four people throws out about $1,600 in rotten food every year. Wow. That makes my head spin! Even if that number is far less in your home, consider these simple ways all of us can stop throwing our food dollars into the garbage.

Freshness Guide

Fresh produce is not cheap, and it's getting more expensive every day—or so it seems. Now more than ever, it's important to bone up on how long your produce purchases are going to last so you make sure no fruits and vegetables end up in the garbage or compost.

You can count on these items to be generally fresh for:

ONE TO THREE DAYS

- Asparagus.
- Berries.
- Fresh leafy greens.
- Peaches.

THREE TO SIX DAYS

- Avocados.
- Bananas.
- Broccoli.
- Green beans.
- Tomatoes.

ONE WEEK OR LONGER

- Apples.
- Carrots.
- Cauliflower.
- Potatoes.
- Squash.

Don't Overbuy

The way to do this is to have a good, realistic plan for the produce you bring into your house. Make certain you will consume it before it goes bad—regardless of the great sale price or how beautiful it looks in the store or farmer's market. Simply buying too much is the number one reason that household produce lands in the garbage.

Disinfect the Fridge

I plead guilty on this one. I just don't think about it if I can't see a mess. The truth is that anytime something spoils in the refrigerator, it leaves behind mold we can't see. As a result, this mold attacks the new, fresh stuff you put in there. Disinfecting the inside surfaces of your refrigerator on a regular schedule will make everything last a little longer and smell a lot better.

Extend Berry Life

Soaking berries in a weak vinegar and water solution before you store them in the refrigerator will make them last for several days longer than simply putting them in the fridge. Add 1 part vinegar to 10 parts water. Swirl the berries around for just a few seconds. Rinse, and store. Strawberries can last up to two weeks longer using this method.

Foodsaver

A FoodSaver vacuum-sealing machine is a great option for extending the useful life of produce. Food can be vacuum-sealed in bags or stored in specific FoodSaver canisters. However, my favorite method for storing everything from strawberries to tomatoes and everything between is in ordinary glass canning jars.

This requires a Jar Sealing Kit that attaches to the FoodSaver. Simply fill a glass canning jar (regular or wide-mouth) with unwashed produce like strawberries, blueberries, tomatoes, lettuce, etc. Set the lid on the jar, and apply the jar sealer. Start the machine and it removes all of the air from the jar and seals the jar tightly.

Stored in the refrigerator, the contents will remain fresh and beautiful for weeks.

Ugly Produce

There are now several companies, such as Imperfect Produce and Misfits Market, that offer a subscription delivery service for "ugly" food. They offer perfectly healthy and nutritious "ugly" produce for up to 50% less than retail store prices. Check this out if nutrition, not perfection, is your goal.

Grow Your Own

Now more than ever, it's important that we think about growing our own food. There's nothing like a worldwide pandemic, long lines at food stores and fear of food shortages to wake us up to the idea of becoming more self-reliant. You don't need acreage to grow a garden. In fact, you don't even need a yard or plot of land (although that is surely a blessing if you do have that).

Start reading; start learning; start a garden!

How to Make Fabulous Meals Using a Formula, Not a Recipe

Ever feel like a kitchen klutz? Wish you could take that odd assortment of stuff in the pantry and freezer, mix it with leftovers in the fridge, and make something delicious without a recipe and without running to the market? That's called cooking with a formula—not a recipe.

Well, grab your whisk, and shout for joy! Thanks to this foolproof five-step formula, you can create fabulous, original and nutritious casseroles designed by YOU, using the items you have on hand.

Step 1: Combine 3/4 cup sour cream, 1 cup milk, 1 cup water, 1 teaspoon salt and 1 teaspoon pepper with one item from Group A, which is coming up below (omit sour cream and milk when using tomatoes).

Step 2: Stir in one item from each of Groups B, C, D and E (again, no sour cream or milk when using tomatoes).

Step 3: Spoon mixture into a lightly greased 13-by-9-by-2-inch baking dish.

Step 4: Sprinkle with one or two choices from Group F.

Step 5: Cover, and bake the casserole at 350 F for 1 hour and 10 minutes. Uncover, and bake 10 additional minutes. Servings: About 6.

Group A:

1 can cream of mushroom soup, undiluted

1 can cream of celery soup, undiluted

1 can cheddar cheese soup, undiluted

2 cans Italian-style diced tomatoes, undrained

1 can cream of chicken soup, undiluted

Don't care for canned soups? Make it yourself! Simply go online and search "how to make homemade cream of anything soup," and you'll find many recipes to choose from.

Group B:

2 cans solid white tuna, drained and flaked

2 cups cooked chicken, chopped

2 cups cooked ham, chopped
2 cups cooked turkey, chopped
1 pound ground beef, browned and drained

Group C:

2 cups uncooked elbow macaroni
1 cup uncooked rice
4 cups uncooked wide egg noodles
3 cups uncooked medium pasta shells

Group D:

1 package chopped spinach, thawed
1 package frozen, cut broccoli
1 package frozen Italian green beans
1 package frozen peas
1 package frozen sliced yellow squash
1 package frozen, whole-kernel corn
Note: packages should be about 10 ounces.

Group E:

1 small can sliced mushrooms, drained
1/4 cup ripe olives, sliced
1/4 cup bell pepper, chopped
1/4 cup onion, chopped
1/4 cup celery, chopped
2 cloves garlic, minced
1 small can chopped green chiles
1 packet taco seasoning mix

Group F:

1/2 cup mozzarella cheese, shredded
1/2 cup Swiss cheese, shredded
1/2 cup Parmesan cheese, grated
1/2 cup fine, dry breadcrumbs

Example Combinations

Chicken Bake: Cream of chicken soup, broccoli, rice, chicken, Parmesan cheese and breadcrumbs.

Ham Casserole: Cream of celery soup, Italian green beans, wide egg noodles, ham, garlic and two portions Swiss cheese.

Turkey Bake: Italian-style diced tomatoes, spinach, medium

pasta shells, turkey, onion, garlic, mozzarella cheese and breadcrumbs.

Vegetarian Casserole: Italian-style diced tomatoes, yellow squash, rice, olives, four portions (1 cup) celery, four portions (ditto) bell pepper, garlic, Parmesan cheese and breadcrumbs.

Now it's your turn!

How to Prevent Cheese From Turning Green and Moldy

Call me picky, but I prefer my greens to be those of the garden variety, not those growing on my cheese.

Don't you just hate when that happens? You buy a block of cheese and before you can use it up, it turns into something that looks more like a science fair project than a tasty dairy product.

I'll admit it. Back in my carefree spendthrift days, I'd toss the cheese in the garbage when it turned moldy. Ick. I was oblivious to the fact that I might as well be throwing dollar bills away.

True, we could opt for buying just a few slices at a time from the deli counter, but that's too expensive. And unnecessary. I can save more than $2 a pound off the best price at the supermarket if I buy in bulk from a discount warehouse like Sam's Club or Costco. And that presents a storage challenge.

Whoever said, "An ounce of prevention is worth a pound of cure," must have been a deli owner. Think about it. With all that cheese in those cases, have you ever seen one growing green mold? Never.

All I know about the proper care and handling of cheese I learned from one such person. That kind deli owner introduced me to the two archenemies of cheese: air and bacteria.

Ounce of Prevention

Air. Limit exposure to air and you can greatly extend the life of any type of cheese. Keep hard cheeses like cheddar or Monterey Jack tightly wrapped with plastic wrap.

Bacteria. We know that it takes bacteria to make cheese in the first place, but that is much different than the kind of bacteria on your hands.

Rule No. 1 of Mold Prevention: Each time you open it, reseal it as tightly and completely as possible. That takes care of the air problem.

Rule No. 2: Don't touch the cheese! Even when you wash your hands well, some amount of bacteria remains, and while it's not at all harmful to you or the cheese, that's what gets that green thing going.

Either wear food preparation gloves or make sure the plastic is always creating a barrier between your hands and the portion of the cheese that's going back into the refrigerator.

Pound of Cure

For cheese that has already turned, there are a couple of remedies.

Vinegar. You can actually wipe the mold away with a clean cloth you've dipped into white vinegar. Not the most pleasant job, but it does work to save the cheese.

Cut it out. Another useful technique is to simply cut away the moldy parts. Once all the green is gone, treat this as you would a new block of cheese by following the two rules above.

Bonus. I'll close today's column with a bonus tip that will at least double the shelf life of cottage cheese. Once opened, stir in a pinch of salt. That slows the growth of bacteria without affecting the taste. Seal the lid, and then store it upside down in the refrigerator. This will seal out the air.

Chicken Labeling at the Supermarket: Prepare to Be Surprised

If you've ever stood in the supermarket wondering if paying more for chicken that is free-range, antibiotic-free, no hormones added, farm-raised, natural and organic is going to make you healthier, wealthier, wise—or just a better person—you're not alone.

Recently, as I was doubting myself on my chicken choices, I decided to get to the bottom of what all of this really means. It's not what I thought.

The U.S. Department of Agriculture is a cabinet-level agency that oversees the regulation of food-grade chicken and is responsible for the claims on packaging and labels.

And despite all of the hype and fluff, there is only one label—organic—that guarantees specific standards and for which you might consider paying more.

Briefly, here is what all of it means—or doesn't mean—according to the USDA.

Free-Range

There is no specific definition for free-range. For sure, it does not mean, "running free to forage for grubs and grain on acres of rolling green pastureland."

The USDA generally allows this term if chickens have access to the outdoors for at least part of the day, which could mean a matter of a few minutes, whether that chicken chooses to go outdoors or not.

A single open door at one end of a huge chicken warehouse meets this definition of free-range. Even so, "Less than 1% of chickens nationwide are raised free-range," according to the National Chicken Council.

Cage-Free

This means not housed in cages. It does not mean roaming happily in large open areas. Cage-free can mean crammed together in an indoor henhouse and given very little room to breathe and be their naturally born chicken selves.

Natural

Under USDA regulations, a "natural" product has no artificial ingredients or added color. Most ready-to-cook chicken can be labeled "natural" if processors choose to do so.

No Hormones Added

This label is meaningless because federal regulations prohibit the use of hormones in chicken. Period.

Any cut or brand of chicken can be labeled "raised without hormones."

However, if the processor chooses to say that on the label, it must also clearly state that no hormones are used in the production of any poultry allowed for consumption in the U.S.

Antibiotic-Free (Or Raised Without Antibiotics)

This means that the flock was raised without the use of products classified as antibiotics for animal health maintenance, disease prevention or treatment of disease.

But why mention this on the label? All processed chickens in the U.S. must be "antibiotic-free" in the sense that no antibiotic residues are allowed to be present in the meat.

Made in the USA

Nearly all chickens and chicken products sold in the U.S. come from chickens hatched, raised and processed in the U.S. An exception is a small number imported from Canada, which has food safety and quality standards equal to the U.S.

Organic

The USDA has a very specific rule to define "organic" production and prohibits the use of the term "organic" on the packaging of any food product not produced in accordance with its rule.

Organic chicken means that 100% of the chicken feed was grown without chemical fertilizers, herbicides and other genetically modified organisms for at least three years.

According to USDA, the organic label does not indicate that the product has safety, quality or nutritional attributes that are any higher than conventionally raised chicken.

Money and Finances: Banks, Credit Cards and More

4 Good Reasons to Kick the Credit Card Habit

There are many reasons not to carry credit card debt. The most obvious is that it's really expensive. And here's a reason often overlooked: It seems so much harder to work for money you've already spent.

But what if you do not carry any credit card debt at all? There are some who would say it is perfectly reasonable to use credit to pay for everything, provided you are able to pay it back down to $0 during the grace period.

Sure, that makes for easy record-keeping, plus all those points, miles and cash rewards that many credit card issuers offer. Even so, it's a habit that can have a negative effect on your financial situation.

You need to kick the credit card habit for these simple reasons:

Your Credit Score

The more you use your cards, the more likely you are to make a mistake. All activity—good or bad—is reported to the credit bureaus and lands in your credit file. That information is then compiled into a three-digit number that can change daily—and be used to determine how much interest you will pay on your mortgage, what your insurance premiums will be and even if you'll get the apartment or job you've applied for.

Credit scores—like it or not—have become a kind of character reference. If your score could use a little help, kick the credit card habit and your credit score is likely to improve all on its own.

According to Credit Karma, "FICO score ranges vary—they can range from 300 to 850 or 250 to 900, depending on the scoring model—but higher scores can indicate that you may be less risky to lenders (and others)."

To get a rough idea of your FICO credit score, you can use the FICO Score Estimator. The calculator is free. Or you can purchase your credit score from https://www.MyFICO.com. On the FICO score range, anything over 740 is good. Higher than 760 is great.

Your Happiness

One study from the Institute for Research on Poverty and the Center for Financial Security at the University of Wisconsin-Madison shows that people with credit card debt and overdue bills are much more likely to experience symptoms of depression than those who don't have such debts, particularly if they are near retirement, unmarried or less educated. The more short-term debt a person had, the more frequently they reported feeling those symptoms.

No surprises there. The effects of credit card debt can be debilitating, if not devastating. But the good news is that kicking the habit allows you to retrace your steps and work your way out of debt. Each repaid debt returns your options. And once out of debt, your peace of mind will return as well. It's not impossible.

In fact, thousands reading this right now have done that using the system I created and you can use. Look for the "Rapid-Debt Repayment Plan" in chapter seven of my book "Debt-Proof Living."

Your Cash

A study from the Massachusetts Institute of Technology called "Always Leave Home Without It: A Further Investigation of the Credit-Card Effect on Willingness to Pay" establishes the fact that people who pay with plastic just spend more—whether it's a soda machine with a credit card slot or a great sale at Target.

If you're paying with plastic, you just feel freer at the moment to load up the tab. But kick the credit card habit, and leave the plastic at home; you will spend less. That means more cash in your pocket.

Your Shelter

It's become the popular thing to tap into one's home equity by way of a home equity loan or refinance to pay off credit card debt. But that's just a way of moving that debt to one's home. The homeowner-borrower puts his or her home at risk should something happen that makes it impossible to keep up with those new, big monthly payments.

Even worse, perhaps, most people who pay off their credit cards turn around and run them back to the max within just two years, getting themselves into double trouble.

Kick the credit card habit and you won't be tempted to tap into this appreciating asset to pay for stuff you charged a long time ago and possibly don't even remember now.

How to Build a Great Credit Score

If you are a legal adult U.S. resident, somewhere there is a three-digit number between 300 and 850 with your name on it. Your credit score measures your creditworthiness, which is the likelihood that you will pay your bills.

Establishing good credit has never been as important to your life as it is today.

You need a good score to get decent mortgages rates, finance a car, get a good job, rent an apartment and find affordable insurance. The way you handle your money has been found to be a very good indicator for how you handle other areas of your life.

A low score doesn't necessarily mean you are a total deadbeat when it comes to handling your money. It could mean you are young and your credit file has your name on it, and that's about it. Here are reasonable ways that you can build a killer credit score quickly.

No 1: Review Your Credit Report

You need to make sure that all of the information in your credit file is correct. This information is available free at the only government-sanctioned credit-reporting-agency-operated website, Annualcreditreport.com, or by calling 1-877-322-8228. Dispute anything on your report that is not correct. If you want to get a copy of your FICO credit score, you'll have to pay a few bucks to get it at https://www.MyFico.com.

No. 2: Open Both a Checking and Savings Account

You receive credit points for financial stability, and having open and working bank accounts contributes to that, even though banks do not report account activity to the credit reporting agencies.

No. 3: Apply for Credit While You're in College

Card companies mostly waive their typical qualifications for college students, which makes it easy to qualify for a credit card.

No. 4: Get a Secured Credit Card

If you can't qualify for a traditional credit card, apply for a secured account. You will have to deposit money with the lender, which will be held in a savings account. Find a list of available secured cards at indexcreditcards.com.

No. 5: Piggyback on Another's Good Credit

If a family member, like a parent, is willing, have that person add you as an authorized user on his or her credit card. Doing this will have that person's credit activity on that one card placed on your credit report.

No. 6: Pay Your Bills on Time

All of them, even those that do not report to credit bureaus.

No. 7: Respect the 30% Threshold

Don't charge up your card close to the limit at any time during the billing cycle, even if you pay the balance in full each month. Keep your use below 30% of your available credit at all times. Crossing that will cause your credit score to drop like a stone!

How to Get Back at Your Creditors

Late fees, punitive interest rates, over-limit fees, loading up your credit report with negative information—it's enough to make you scream!

It's not that your creditors are doing anything illegal. You just didn't understand the power you gave them when you accepted that credit card. It was buried in the fine print. And now, it seems like they're staying up all night looking for new ways to stick it to you. If you've just about had enough, maybe it's time for you to turn the tables and get back at them.

Pay Early

According to industry research organization R.K. Hammer, in 2016, credit card companies hauled in $163 billion, 30% of which was derived from annual fees, late fees, and over-limit fees. You'd think they would be pretty satisfied with all that interest you send them each month. But no. They want more. The days when issuers allowed 10 or 15 days for a payment to arrive after a due date before charging a fee are long gone. Now, those fees kick in if you're even five minutes late, and can be as high as $39 per occurrence.

Get back at your credit card company by making the decision right now to never pay another dime in late fees. Be quick with your payment. Send it in the prepaid envelope that came with your statement—or pay online. Don't enclose a note. Use a paper clip, decorate it with stickers or do anything that will pull it out of the fast track and into manual processing.

Stay Below

Your credit card account most likely has a credit limit. But running up a balance that is anywhere near that limit is deadly for your credit score. The rule of thumb is that you should never be using more than 30% of your credit limit. For example, if your limit is $1,000, you should never have a balance of more than $300. Zero balance is even better!

Get back at your card company by creating a wide margin between your balance and your limit.

Stop Using

Your card companies are playing the odds. They know the more you use your cards, the better their chances that you'll go nuts and rack up a big load of debt. When your balance becomes greater than the amount you can pay off in a single month, they've got you. They're doing all they can to encourage that to happen.

Get back at your company by not adding new purchases to your burgeoning load of debt. You'll do yourself a favor and get back at them at the same time.

Open Eyes

All of your creditors know what's in your credit report. They read it regularly. You should too. Part of your agreement with them is that they can check up on you whenever they like to see how you are handling your financial affairs.

Get back at your creditors by staying ahead of them. Manage your credit report by reading it regularly. You can get it for free at AnnualCreditReport.com. If you don't understand what it says, ask. And if you see something on there that you know to be untrue, dispute. But don't stop there. If your creditors are punishing you for things on your credit report that were not true, don't sit back passively. Dispute those errors. Don't back off until they reverse the action.

Pay Off

Probably nothing will benefit you more than bringing your balances to $0. It's like getting a tax-free raise because you get to keep all of that money you've been sending each month to your creditors.

Get back at your creditors by refusing to send them one more penny in interest or penalty fees.

The Most Overlooked Type of Insurance

Insurance is a funny thing. You learn all you can, shop diligently, scrape together the money to pay for it and then hope you'll never have to use it.

In addition to health and automobile coverage, most people insure their lives so that in the event of their death, those who depend on their income will not be left high and dry.

Term life insurance, the insurance of choice for all us cheapskates, is relatively cheap because so many people pay for it who never use it. The insurance companies invest all of those premiums, make an obscene fortune doing so and end up paying out far less than they take in.

Face it, folks: These days, with medical technology what it is, the odds increase every day that a disease or accident that would have killed you a decade ago will now leave you disabled—alive but unable to work.

Unfortunately, many of us will need disability income protection sometime before we die. One out of every 4 of today's 20-year-olds will be incapacitated for at least a year before they reach age 65. Without insurance, a disability could spell financial disaster.

A recent study reported in the American Journal of Public Health found that 66.5% of all bankruptcies in the U.S. (approximately 530,000 households per year) were due to medical issues—either because of high costs of medical care, time out of work or both.

Why It's So Expensive

Disability insurance is far more expensive than term life insurance. In fact, it rivals the more-expensive whole life insurance but does not offer the dubious advantage of cash values. No wonder so many people overlook this most important of all insurances.

Disability insurance is relatively expensive because there's a much higher probability you will use it. With life insurance, most people underestimate their life span, so they end up buying insurance they will never use. Or they buy ridiculously expensive insurance. such as whole life or universal life, and then drop it the minute they go through a financial downturn.

But when it comes to disabilities, people of all ages have equal risks, which means it is more likely you will need it at some time. If you are in a two-breadwinner household, it is likely you need disability insurance more than life insurance, given how expensive it can be to care for a disabled person.

How It Works

Standard disability insurance is fairly straightforward. If you are unable to work and are found disabled as defined by the policy, the insurance company replaces a specific percentage of the income you would have earned had you not been disabled.

In the same way that health, auto and life insurance policies have unique provisions, exclusions and stipulations, there are all kinds of provisions in a disability policy that you should consider carefully. Generally speaking, the lower the premium, the greater the number of exclusions and stipulations. Consider them carefully, and never consider anything you do not fully understand.

What To Look For

No. 1: Guaranteed and noncancelable. This type of policy will have a fixed premium and will stay in effect as long as your payments are kept current, regardless of health issues or other variables.

No. 2: Insures for your occupation. Make sure your policy protects you against your inability to work in your own occupation; otherwise, your insurer will not pay you unless you can't work at all.

No. 3: Payment increases. You want a rider on your policy that provides for payment increases to keep up with inflation and also in sync with your income. If you bought the policy when you made $25,000 and make $85,000 when you suffer a disability, you want to make sure you are covered at the $85,000 level.

No. 4: Pays until retirement. Some disability policies pay for only a specific period of time, say, five or 10 years. The best policy is open-ended and continues as long as you are disabled, until retirement age.

Even if you feel you are not in a position to take on another expense at this time, think about it. Do yourself a favor and find out what it would cost. Ask friends or relatives for a referral to an agent or disability insurance carrier. Query your current insurance carrier. It will cost you nothing to do the homework.

Overspent and Overloaded? You Need Margin

Bill Smith sits down to his most dreaded chore–paying bills. Every month, it's the same story: Pay the most urgent, and leave the rest. There's never enough money, no matter how hard he works.

Jane Miller flies into the school office frazzled and 30 minutes late because she was 20 minutes late getting out of the dentist's office because she was 15 minutes late to her appointment. How will she ever get the kids home, homework started and dinner on the table, and be back out the door in time to chair the PTA meeting that evening?

Tom Johnson gets up every morning at 4:30 to make the 5:30 train for his 90-minute commute into the city. He crams during every spare minute for the classes he's taking at night. Getting his degree is no longer something Tom can put off.

It's been weeks since Tom's made it home for dinner. But what's he to do? Without a promotion, they will never make it on a single salary. His ever-growing student debt will come due whether he graduates or not. Quitting is out of the question. Most days, it is all Tom can do to just keep going.

Bill's, Jane's and Tom's situations could not be more different. Yet they share the same problem. They are stretched to the limit.

Bill is living beyond 120% of his income; Jane is presuming upon more than 120% of her time, and Tom is requiring more than 120% of his energy. All are overspent and overloaded and perfect candidates for all kinds of stress-related maladies.

Richard A. Swenson, M.D., author of the book "Margin," explains: "Margin is that space between us and our limits. It's something held in reserve for contingencies or unanticipated situations. As a society, we've forgotten what margin is. In the push for progress, margin has been devoured. We are besieged by anxiety, stress and fatigue. Our relationships suffer. We have unexplained aches and pains. The flood of daily events seems beyond our control. We are overloaded!"

Most people regularly commit to a 120% life. It's rare these days to see a life prescheduled to only 80%, leaving a margin for responding to the unexpected, says Swenson.

Pain characterizes the marginless life. Physical, emotional and spiritual pain is manifested in many different ways, such as increased blood pressure, chest pain, arrhythmias, hyperacidity, ulcers, back pain, headaches, fatigue, depression, withdrawal, confusion, worry, teeth grinding, jaw-clenching, compulsive shopping, hostility, paranoia, insomnia, burnout, breakdown, addictions–need I go on?

The way to build margin into our lives is to simplify. That means downscaling, dejunking, reducing expenses and choosing to say no so we can give ourselves the gift of margin.

Life is too short to live stretched beyond the limit. If you yearn for relief from the pain and pressure of overload, Swenson suggests a daily dose of margin. The benefits of good health, financial stability, fulfilling relationships, peace and joy are what you can expect for your efforts.

Sneaky Ways to Save Big

I blame it on my friend Kathleen that I caught the sneaky savings bug. One day, years ago, she told me her secret. Whenever she wrote a check, she'd enter an incorrect amount in the register by rounding up to the next dollar–sometimes five. Once a year, she'd reconcile her account and discover, to her utter joy, enough "found" money in the account to pay for Christmas. Brilliant!

Saving money in sneaky ways is all about timing and discipline mixed with a healthy dose of courage. It's learning how to fly under the radar to save money in ways others might not think about. You have to pay close attention and read all of the fine print, too.

Good Rooms, Cheap

Don't call the toll-free reservation number when you need to book a hotel room, advises travel expert Peter Greenberg. You'll speak with a reservations operator who has no wiggle room to give you a discounted rate. Instead, Greenberg recommends waiting until Sunday around 4 p.m. local time to call the hotel directly. Why? Typically, that's when the hotel revenue managers who usually set and control the room rates are not working. Ask to speak with a manager or supervisor. Now you have the ear of a person with whom you can negotiate the price.

Deals on Meds

These days, the high cost of prescription medications is enough to make you sick–even if you have insurance that picks up some of the cost. Here's a little-known tactic to whittle down the price. Before you go to the pharmacy, go to the website for that medication to check for coupons and rebates you can use to reduce your copay. An example: the Nasonex website offers a printable coupon for up to $10 off, and you can come back every 30 days to print out an additional savings coupon for your refill–up to $120 a year with the Personalized Savings Program. Lipitor also has a similar offer. You may have to click around the site to find the deals, and offers can change frequently, but being diligent and checking back often can save you hundreds.

New Car Holdout

To get the best bargain on a new car, be patient, says James Bragg, auto expert and founder of car buying and leasing company Fighting Chance. The best week of the year to make a great deal is the week between Christmas and New Year's. It's the end of the month, end of the quarter and end of the year–and these are all aligned for the only time all year. Also, dealers are much more flexible about pricing. It's the one time that you'll get in on a car buyer's rock-bottom market!

Whack the Interest

Take a load of interest off your home mortgage and pay off your house years early by adding one-twelfth of a mortgage payment to your principal each month. As long as you do not have a prepayment penalty, the lender will accept more than the required payment and will apply this to the principal, per your instructions to do so. Refer to this amount as a "principal prepayment." This may not seem like much, but the effect is huge. Every 12 months, you'll make the equivalent of 13 mortgage payments–one extra payment a year.

Here's an example: Let's say you bought a house for $170,000 at a 6% interest rate fixed for 30 years. The monthly payment is $1,019.23. One-twelfth is $84.94–the amount you'll pay each month in addition to your regular payment. Sticking to this plan, you would pay off your 30-year mortgage in 24 years and five months, and as a bonus, you would save $41,746.69 in interest charges.

How to Automate Your Finances

I once flew in a chartered jet, not exactly like a rock star, but I did feel quite pampered. The flight was awesome, but I have to admit to momentarily freaking out when the pilot unbuckled his seatbelt, stood up, left the pilot seat and came back to chat with his three passengers over snacks and sodas.

While he sat with us for more than an hour, it took only a few minutes for me to relax and enjoy the company and the ride.

Relying on autopilot in both flying and finances is quite an amazing thing.

Creditors, especially banks and credit card issuers, are unbelievably sensitive to whether you pay your bills on time. So is your credit score. One slip-up could cost you dearly if it means you lose your low interest rate or no interest rate, or if a late payment results in a big late fee.

Late payments are reported to the credit bureaus, and that can mean a serious blow to your credit score, which may result in higher insurance premiums now and higher interest rates on your next mortgage. If you're thinking "domino effect," you are exactly right. Bottom line: Do not pay late!

An excellent way to make sure you always pay on time is to automate (sometimes referred to as auto bill pay).

By putting your payments on auto pay, you eliminate that monthly decision: Should I pay bills tonight or wait until Tuesday? Should I put money into savings this month or buy those cute shoes?

For me, the fewer financial decisions I have to make on a daily basis, the better. That's why I love automatic payments.

There are several ways to do this, but all result in the same thing: Your finances are set to autopilot while you are off enjoying life.

You can set up auto payments two ways:

Online Bill Pay

Use your bank's online bill pay option, which is a free service at most banks but also at credit unions, brokerages and mutual fund accounts. An automatic bill payment is a money transfer from your account on a predetermined date or schedule, to pay a recurring bill.

Automatic payments can be made from a checking account or credit card. They are usually set up with the company receiving the payment, though it's also possible to schedule automatic payments through a checking account online bill pay service.

Banks don't all operate exactly the same way, so go online to check out your bank's auto bill pay service.

Automatic Authorized Payments

Most lenders and other service providers will let you set up an online automatic payment that authorizes them to reach into your checking account right before the payment is due each month and take an amount you specify–the minimum payment, a set dollar amount or the full balance.

Go to your credit card issuer's and other lenders' websites to learn more.

Most utility companies now offer this kind of service, too. And while we're talking about it, if you set up your student loans to be paid automatically, expect to get a reduction in your interest rate as a nice thank you. Check it out.

Bonus

Not so keen on automating your bills and payments? You can use this method and process in another way–to automate your savings!

Set up an automatic authorization at your bank or credit union to have a set amount of money transferred from your checking account, where you deposit your paychecks, into your savings account. Start small, if you must, but just do it. It will change things for you, and I mean in a really awesome way.

Here's what will happen: The first time the money is moved, you'll feel panicked because you'll feel the loss. Buck up. Dry your tears. You'll be just fine.

The second time this happens, you will be slightly agitated. But the third, fourth and on and on? You will totally forget it happens! Trust me on this. Now and then when you think of it and check your savings balance, you will rejoice. And thank me.

You Need a Freedom Account

If I asked you to deduct your monthly expenses from your monthly income, I have a feeling you'd look pretty good on paper. The mystery for many people is why they can't get through a month without using a credit card to cover unexpected expenses, such as a prescription for a sick child, a quarterly insurance premium or a wedding shower gift.

Your predictable, fixed monthly bills are not the problem. Somehow, the rent and utilities get paid, and the family gets fed. The problem is the accumulation of nonmonthly expenses. Some are easily predictable; others are not.

Here's the problem: Every day, we are wearing out our cars, the kids are growing out of their shoes, we're using up our prepaid insurance, and we're inching closer to the holidays and vacation. But we manage our money as if none of those things is ever going to happen. And when they do, we collapse into a pitiful heap and bemoan the fact that, once again, we've been broadsided by an emergency—another financial crisis!

The solution for this problem is to establish what I call a "freedom account" that forces you to anticipate unexpected, irregular and intermittent expenses and finance your own emergencies.

Step No. 1: Determine Irregular Expenses

Using your check registers for the past 12 months, your credit card statements, your tax return or, if all else fails, your memory, make a list of expenses you've had over the last year that you did not pay on a monthly basis. It might be insurance, property taxes, Little League fees, gifts, clothing, vacation, Christmas, car repairs, sports, hobbies, etc.

Come up with an annual figure (estimate if you don't know), and then divide by 12 so you arrive at a figure that represents one-twelfth of the total annual expense.

For example:

Auto maintenance: $900/12 = $75

Auto insurance: $540/12 = $45

Christmas: $800/12 = $66
Property taxes: $600/12 = $50
Vacation: $720/12 = $60
Clothing: $600/12 = $50
Total: $346

Step No. 2: Open Another Checking Account

It's easiest if you open this at your current bank or credit union. Order checks for this new account, and have them personalized, including a line that says "freedom account." You need two active checking accounts for this to work. Your regular checking account will continue to accommodate your monthly expenses and deposits.

Step No. 3: Authorize an Automatic Deposit

At the time you open this account, request an automatic deposit or money transfer authorization form. Fill it out, instructing the bank to transfer the monthly total of your irregular expenses (in our example, it is $346) from your regular checking account into your freedom account every month on the same day.

Step No. 4: Get a Notebook

Any three-ring binder will do. Fill it with paper. Prepare one page per subaccount you've chosen. Fill in the title of the subaccounts that you established in Step No. 1. Enter the amount to be deposited into that subaccount each month in the upper righthand corner. Prepare five columns for each subaccount: "date," "description," "in," "out" and "balance."

Step No. 5: Manage Your Freedom Account

You now have a new regular monthly expense; in this case, it is $346. This is going to feel weird in the beginning. The truth is you are managing your money in a new way that puts you in control and reduces your dependence on credit.

Each month when that automatic money transfer happens, go to your freedom account notebook and enter the deposits on each page so you always know how much you have in each subaccount.

At times, you will be tempted to think of this new account as a savings account or investment holding tank. This is not a savings account. It's a management account from which you are going to pay your irregular expenses using the checkbook you got when you opened it.

You may be tempted to skip funding your savings or emergency fund in favor of your freedom account. Do not do that. Scrimp wherever you must to free up funds for your freedom account every month while continuing to grow your savings.

Your new freedom account will give new meaning to the term "ebb and flow." It will accumulate big balances and then drop to hardly anything. But that's the way it's supposed to work. It is strictly a financial management tool that is going to make you feel confident and very grown up.

Don't be hesitant to establish lots of subaccounts, even if you are unable to fund all of them in the beginning. It's OK to have pages with zero balances for now, so dream big. Design with the future in mind!

A Couple's Guide to Common Money Myths

The wedding was beautiful and fulfilled your fondest dreams. But it's over, and now it's time to settle in and enjoy your new life together. Lucky for you, I'm here to warn you about some common money myths that newlyweds have been known to bring with them into their marriages.

Myth: Double the Income, Half the Expenses

This is what I call newlywed fuzzy math: Merging your lives and incomes into one household is the equivalent of getting a raise. Don't believe that, not for a second.

Counter: Start out living on only one income, and save the rest. This will require going against everything the culture insists you deserve, but it will allow you to move seamlessly into parenthood. When that day comes, you'll have an impressive savings account and options. And a gallery of envious friends.

Myth: There's Stuff We Can't Live Without

No, there isn't. But it will be easy to convince yourselves that you absolutely must have matching furniture, new cars, and all kinds of gadgets and services to make your lives easier and keep up with your friends.

Counter: Make a pact that you will never go into debt for "stuff." Period.

Myth: If We Qualify, We Can Afford It

Whether it's a new credit card or a new nothing-down, interest-only mortgage for a house that, in your hearts, you know you cannot afford, never allow your ability to qualify to be the determining factor. Getting in over your heads in a house or credit card debt is the recipe for a marital disaster.

Counter: Never think of a credit card company, real estate agent or mortgage broker as a financial adviser. They are salespeople looking to close deals. Get advice from a wise person who will not benefit financially from the decision you make.

Myth: We Have Plenty of Time

It does seem as though you have a lifetime ahead. And that you don't really need to save money now, while things are tight.

But that's a myth.

The truth is you cannot afford to go one more day without a savings commitment for many reasons. You will want to retire. You do not want to feel forced into debt when something unexpected happens. You do not want to get used to spending all that you have. You want to create a sense of security and peace in your marriage.

Counter: See 10% of your net income as a mandatory financial obligation, just like your rent or mortgage payment. Pay it to yourselves, without fail, starting now

Myth: Some Money Issues Are Best Kept Private

Whether it's student debt or a secret credit card account, keeping money secrets from your beloved is not good for your marriage. You might be able to pull off financial infidelity for a while, but eventually, it will come back to bite you.

Counter: Start out with a commitment to full disclosure and total honesty. That will build something into your marriage that money cannot buy: trust.

Myth: Everything Will Be Fine As Soon As We Make More Money

It does make sense that if you are struggling now, you won't once you get a big raise or finish school or get your grandmother's inheritance or win the lottery. The truth is that more money will never be enough until you learn how to manage the money you already have.

Counter: Make the necessary adjustments now to live beneath your means. That will ensure that when more money comes into your lives, you'll know exactly how to take care of it.

Myth: It's Too Late

No matter how long you've been married or how difficult your situation may appear, it's not too late. It will take longer and be more challenging, but you can turn your situation around. Two people committed to reaching a single goal create a powerful force.

Counter: Decide right now that you are going to do whatever it takes to debt-proof your marriage!

Kids

6 Things Kids Need To Know About Spending Money

What grade would you give your parents for how well they prepared you to manage your finances? What grade will your kids give you someday?

There are six basic financial principles your kids need to know before they leave the safety net of home.

No. 1: How You Spend Affects Your Future

Kids need to know that if they spend their money without thinking about their choices, they will probably make bad decisions. Teach them how to stop and think before making any spending decision.

No. 2: Create Goals for How You Will Spend Your Money

A goal is like a roadmap. It shows where you are and where you want to go. When setting goals, think short-term, medium-term and long-term. Short-term goals might have something to do with tomorrow. Medium-term could be months or even a year away. Long-term goals are far away. Here's a secret: Until goals are actually written down, they're not goals at all. They're dreams. It's important to get into the habit of writing down goals and following with a plan for how to reach them.

No. 3: Your Values Influence the Way You Spend Money

Your kids' values are more likely caught that taught. What you do speaks louder than what you say. Let them catch you in the act of saving, giving to others and saying words such as "budget" and "savings." Instead of saying, "We can't afford it," say instead, "We don't choose to spend our money that way." Let the kids know that you save first and spend later and that debt is a cruel master.

No. 4: Understand the Difference Between Wants and Needs

Sometimes, it's not easy to tell the difference between a want and a need. A need is something required to sustain life, health or safety, or to comply with a legal obligation. Food, shelter, clothes, medicine and paying taxes are needs. But it can get a little complicated. Are Levi jeans a need or a want? Clothes are a need, but paying a lot of money to get a certain brand crosses over to a want. There is nothing wrong with wanting things. It's important for kids to be crystal-clear on whether something is a need or a want.

No. 5: Opportunity Cost Is Real

What we give up when making a spending decision is called the "opportunity cost." Let's say you have $5. You can save it or spend it. If I choose to spend it, you can do that only once. You lose the opportunity to save it and to derive all the benefits that come with saving. Is that one-time purchase worth the opportunity cost? Train your brain to calculate the opportunity cost of every spending decision and you will start making better choices with your money.

No. 6: You Can't Have It All, but You Can Have Enough

Every day, we make decisions, and many of them involve money. Let the kids know that as they prove they can be responsible with money, they'll have more of it to take care of. Making good decisions with their money now will make their lives much more enjoyable in the future.

Give Your Kids Flying Lessons

Kids of elementary school age are becoming aware of the real world around them. They are eager to learn and still believe everything adults tell them. And they want their own money.

For all of those reasons, I suggest that now is the perfect time to start a simple allowance system. This will create wonderful opportunities for you to pass on your values as you closely guide your young children through simple lessons on giving, needs-versus-wants and delaying gratification.

How Much?

So, how much allowance should a young child receive? The amount depends on your financial situation. Some families set allowance according to age–say, $1 for each year of age. This eliminates questions about when and how much to increase.

How Often?

At this age, kids do better with close supervision and short time frames, so receiving their allowance weekly is best.

Should It Be Tied to Chores?

Many experts say allowance should absolutely be the payment children receive for doing their chores and assigned jobs. No work, no pay.

Others feel that citizens of the "family community" should share in its income and responsibilities. They say an allowance should not be the payment for chores, but they add that with privilege comes responsibility. Citizens must do chores and jobs because they are part of the community. That's what good citizens do.

4-Jar Management

A simple way to teach a child basic money management is to get four jars and label them: "giving," "long-term savings," "short-term savings" and "spend now." Clear plastic containers are best because your child will be able to see how the coins and currency are accumulating, but you won't worry about the hazards glass containers can present.

"Giving" is money your child gives to charity or church.

"Long-term savings" are for college or something far in the future.

"Short-term savings" are for something significant like a new bike or special toy.

"Spend now" is money your child can spend right away.

Using the four-container system, you may decide on a 10-30-30-30 plan, where 10% is designated for giving and 30% each for long-term, short-term and immediate spending. Or you can do 10-30-40-20. Whatever it is, make it nonnegotiable, and then help your children use their math skills while at the same time developing a habit of managing their money before they spend it,

Last, teach your children, "To whom much is given, much is required!" A simple spending journal is a way that children can become accountable for how and where they spend their money.

The goal of parenting is to help children grow wings to eventually fly away. Building financial confidence in your children's lives is one important way you can prepare them for the flight.

You may believe that you have lots of time to deal with the letting-go part of parenting. That may be true, but I can tell you from experience that it will be a lot easier if you start now.

Outfitting Your Kids for School–and Fundraisers, Too

Have I been sleeping in a cave for 100 years? Sure feels like it.

I just read that Americans' back-to-school sales could hit a record $101.6 billion to outfit youngsters and college students for the 2020-2021 school year, according to the National Retail Federation. And by outfitted, I mean with all the proper electronic gear, shoes with all the bells and whistles (like a pair of those sneakers with little wheels embedded in the soles), backpacks and, of course, the ever-popular school supplies.

Yikes! That's a whole lotta money.

Granted, I don't have school-aged children anymore, but come on! Kids in kindergarten through 12th grade will increase their spending from an average of $697 in 2019 to an average of $790. Families with college-aged kids are projected to spend an average of $1,060, up from $977 last school year.

Look, I'm open to being proven wrong, but is this anywhere close to reasonable? Perhaps, if you felt you had to purchase an entire school year's worth of pencils, pens, crayons, paper, notebooks, binders, calculators, printer cartridges, shoes, sneakers, jeans, slacks, sweaters, blouses, shirts, socks and undies. But I find that to be a little ridiculous in that kids do grow, and styles do change–and, quite frankly, who wants to do all that laundry?

Spreading the cost over the school year seems more reasonable to me. Unless it's notebooks, pens and paper. Those are so cheap at the start of a new school year at office supply stores that you would have been smart to stock up for the entire year.

So, am I missing something here? I'd love to go head-on with any school-aged family to prove to them that I could get the kids looking mighty fine with all the stuff they need in their backpacks for a lot less than that published per-child average.

While we're on the subject of school, let's throw fundraisers into the discussion.

Every year, I get a flood of messages that are some variation of: "I am so sick of my kids bringing home catalogs full of cheap, overpriced stuff that the school expects us to sell. How can we deal with this? I'd love some advice and insight on how other parents do it."

I remember those days. Of course, I wanted my kids to win all the prizes for being the best little fundraisers, which multiplied the pressure we already felt from the school and Little League. I pity all of my co-workers, neighbors, relatives and friends who got caught up in my web of obligation.

Personally, I'm married to a guy who is a big old softy when it comes to children bearing boxes of anything that they're selling to raise money for their schools and teams. I think we still have the World's Finest chocolate bars left in the freezer from last season. And probably a tub or two of cookie dough in the freezer, too. Oh, and gift wrap and candles.

Now that I think about it, maybe I haven't moved beyond the fundraiser pressure cooker season of my life after all.

So, how do you deal with fundraisers? I can't think of a better place to unload, share, question or even plead your case for your particular fundraiser of choice than by sending me a message. I'm easy to find here: https://EverydayCheapskate.com/contact. I can't wait to hear from you!

How to Get the Kids' Rooms Organized

Even though most schools have returned to in-person learning, it may feel as if the kids have been home, like, forever–with their rooms nodding in agreement! Perhaps it's time to get the kids' rooms organized!

Don't make their bedrooms a battleground. Instead, grab this opportunity to help your kids organize their rooms and their stuff.

Get Down to Kid Level

Look at your child's room at kids-eye level, and you'll get a new perspective. Their adult-sized dressers may have drawers that are too heavy for little hands to open, and closet doors are rarely designed for a child's height.

To help, remove the closet doors and lids from all storage containers and toy boxes. In the closet, lower the clothes rod to your child's height. Use child-sized hangers, and get baskets to house socks and underwear.

Let the Kids Participate

Rather than using the bulldozer approach–where Mom or Dad comes through with a big trash bag and indiscriminately cleans up–get the kids involved. Help them survey and divide their things into three categories:

- Use now.
- Want to keep.
- Don't want anymore.

Try to advise rather than control the situation. Let the kids suggest ways to make a place for everything so everything can be in its place.

Get Hooked

Hooks are the way to create a place for all kinds of things that can so easily get lost and forgotten at the bottom of a junk drawer. Or forever lost in a big pile in the closet.

Place the hook at the child's eye level, complete with a label or picture next to it for what belongs on that hook. You'll be amazed at how quickly your kids begin to identify a hook and its color with the item that belongs on it.

Sort and Store

Rather than keeping every toy in their rooms, help the kids separate their toys and put some away in "storage" in another part of the house. Every month or two, swap toys in their room for some toys in storage.

Once you know what will stay in your child's room, it's time to sort according to colors and like items.

Start with the clothes, and then move to the toys and games.

Plastic Storage Boxes

Clear plastic shoe boxes are great for all the little things like tiny doll clothes, crayons, Legos, CDs and video games. They're clear, so the kiddos can see what is inside and what is supposed to be in there. They're also sturdy and just the right size; even when loaded to the top, the kids can lift to take them in and out, quite easily.

Large bins with lids removed work the same way. Store picture books standing upright in a plastic dishpan. Even preschoolers can flip through to find the book they want without pulling down an entire shelf in the process.

Inexpensive cardboard magazine holders (available at an office supply store) are perfect to keep magazines, comic books and other similarly sized papers so they're neatly stored but easily accessible.

Label Everything

Once you have everything sorted and stored, start labeling. There are lots of ways to create labels. The important thing is that the label means something to the child, regardless of his or her age.

For little ones, cut out pictures that indicate what goes in this box or container. For children who can read, make labels on your computer using big, bold letters that leave no question about what lives on this hook, in this container or on that shelf.

The secret to organizing a child's room is to make it at least as easy to put something away as it was to get it out. When you involve your child in the process of organizing and making decisions, you can be sure your child will be more eager to learn and exercise his or her organizational skills to keep it that way.

About the Author

With many years of successful entrepreneurial experience under her belt, Mary Hunt felt ready to take public her credo, "Bringing dignity to the art of living below your means." As creator and editor of Debt-Proof Living (formerly Cheapskate Monthly), a monthly newsletter that premiered in January 1992 to overwhelming success, Mary has combined her expertise in business with a message that over-spenders and those burdened with debt seem ready to hear.

Debt-Proof Living continues to expand its consumer influence and subscriber base, most notably through its electronic family of subscribers via its website, www.debtproofliving.com. The website attracts more than 8 million hits a month and features Mary's constant themes of financial responsibility, empowerment and hope.

In the fall of 2005, Mary joined the editorial team at Woman's Day magazine (20 million readers), as WD's money guru and contributing editor. Her column, Your Money, first appeared in the January 2006 issue and can be found in every issue of the magazine.

Mary also can be seen every weekday in hundreds of newspapers across the country in her Everyday Cheapskate column. Distributed by Creators Syndicate, Mary's column features household tips, money-saving strategies, reader questions and recipes. Debuting in January 2003, Everyday Cheapskate has been embraced by consumers unsure about the economy and looking to tighten their financial belts.

Prior to devoting herself full time to her writing and speaking projects, Mary co-founded the highly regarded and very profitable industrial real estate brokerage and property management firm, Hunt Industrial Properties.

Made in the USA
Monee, IL
08 November 2026

68002517R00090